DATE DUE

GAYLORD			PRINTED IN U.S.A.

D1279880

FOUNDING FATHER

FOUNDING FATHER

How C-SPAN's Brian Lamb Changed Politics in America

STEPHEN E. FRANTZICH

ROWMAN & LITTLEFIELD PUBLISHERS, INC.
Lanham • Boulder • New York • Toronto • Plymouth, UK

ROWMAN & LITTLEFIELD PUBLISHERS, INC.

Published in the United States of America
by Rowman & Littlefield Publishers, Inc.
A wholly owned subsidary of The Rowman & Littlefield Publishing Group, Inc.
4501 Forbes Boulevard, Suite 200, Lanham, Maryland 20706
www.rowmanlittlefield.com

Estover Road
Plymouth PL6 7PY
United Kingdom

Distributed by National Book Network

British Library Cataloguing in Publication Information Available

Library of Congress Cataloging-in-Publication Data

Frantzich, Stephen E.
  Founding father : how C-SPAN's Brian Lamb changed politics in America /
Stephen E. Frantzich.
       p. cm.
  Includes bibliographical references.
  ISBN-13: 978-0-7425-5850-2 (cloth : alk. paper)
  ISBN-10: 0-7425-5850-9 (cloth : alk. paper)
  1. C-SPAN (Television network) 2. Lamb, Brian, 1941– I. Title.
  PN1992.92.C2F73 2008
  384.55'5092—dc22
  [B]   2007042964

Printed in the United States of America

∞™ The paper used in this publication meets the minimum requirements of
American National Standard for Information Sciences—Permanence of Paper for
Printed Library Materials, ANSI/NISO Z39.48-1992.

CONTENTS

ACKNOWLEDGMENTS

At numerous book signings associated with my coauthored 1996 history of C-SPAN (*The C-SPAN Revolution*) the most commonly asked question was, "What is Brian Lamb like?" While dozens of interviews had give me a pretty good idea, there seemed to be considerable appetite among the public. Consistent with his personality, Brian objected to and then demurred initial requests to cooperate with a biography. When finally worn down, he tepidly said, "I don't want it done, but I assume it will be and I would rather have you do it." I took this as a license to proceed. Eventually Brian subjected himself to a number of new interviews, and provided me with a list of friends and family whose insights greatly enhanced the story. Debbie Lamb, Brian's niece, was particularly helpful in arranging interviews in Indiana. Lee Ann Long, C-SPAN archivist, did significant photo research. Authors James Lardner and Michael Leahy turned over dozens of interviews carried out for other purposes. My wife Jane provided her usual editorial tasks and was able to guide me in ways less acceptable from others.

1

INTRODUCTION
A Bridge Spanning the Political Chasm

> We are told never to cross a bridge till we come to it, but this
> world is owned by men who have crossed bridges in their
> imagination far ahead of the crowd.
>
> —Anonymous (Library Speakers)

As a preteen, Brian Lamb often came home from school, jumped on his bike, and ended up at the bicycle bridge a few hundred yards from his Lafayette, Indiana, home. While his life was largely limited to the Shawnee Circle neighborhood, the bridge served a ray of hope that a larger and more exciting world lay beyond. The bridge served as a key focal point, a place to meet friends and a link to kids from other neighborhoods. It became a symbol of a young boy's potential vehicle for exploring new worlds and experiencing them firsthand. As a young boy, his mother warned him, "You can ride anywhere around the neighborhood, but not across the bridge." For a number of years, the forbidden fruit was only tasted when others crossed the bridge to his side. Later, the constraints loosened and the bridge no longer served as a barrier, but rather as an opportunity. While the two neighborhoods linked by the bridge revealed only minute differences, the bridge linked Brian to another set of people, some of whom became lifelong friends. It also symbolized the numerous bridges he might traverse in life. Over fifty years later, the bridge is one of the first places Brian visits when he goes home. He placed a picture of the bridge on the back of one of his books, and a much larger version graces a prominent place in his home.

Bridges often serve to open the horizons of those on both sides. The Chesapeake Bay Bridge opened the Eastern Shore of Maryland to the economics, language, and tourists from the western shore of the Chesapeake. The Golden Gate Bridge made both the inland areas and the city of San Francisco accessible to each other. Building bridges equalizes power, integrates economies, and homogenizes cultures.

The bicycle bridge serves as a symbol of Brian's lifelong role as a bridge builder. His passion was not so much to move people physically, as to open their minds by overcoming parochial outlooks and gaps in their knowledge. What others accomplished with bricks, steel, and mortar, Brian consummated with ideas more than materials. The payload on his bridge focused on politics and information.

ONE GIANT STEP INTO THE UNKNOWN

About twenty-five years after his last childhood ride across the bicycle bridge, Brian ventured out on a much riskier structure. It was not his first attempt at bridge building, but surely stands out as his most audacious. The creation of C-SPAN (the Cable Satellite Public Affairs Network) developed from Brian's desire to bridge the gap between politics in Washington and the kind of friends and neighbors he knew growing up in Lafayette. He recognized that while not necessarily sophisticated about politics, their interest failed to be fed by the existing sources of information. He also had a sneaky suspicion that decision makers in Washington would benefit from a more robust dialogue with average Americans since a gap had developed that needed to be bridged.

"Opening day" has connotations of balloons, banners, and hoopla. The very term of "launching" a new service implies excitement and activity. The first day of coverage of the House of Representatives in the C-SPAN offices dawned like any other business day. While over three million households could now see the House live, the signal did not reach across the Potomac River to C-SPAN's cramped, two-room office in Crystal City, Virginia. Just like most Americans, no one in the C-SPAN office heard Al Gore make the maiden speech extolling "the marriage of the medium and our open debate . . . to revitalize representative democracy."[1]

Only a few hours before the deadline, Brian Lamb was less worried about fulfilling his promise to put the House of Representatives on air gavel-to-gavel than how to get cement poured in the cold Virginia rain, snow, and omnipresent mud. Totally out of his realm, Brian activated his penchant for bridging by calling an old Indiana friend with construction experience in seeking advice on how to get cement trucks through knee-deep mud. In preparation for the big day, Brian spent much of his time sloshing around in the mud trying to get his network on the air. It was an inauspicious beginning for an untrained niche market journalist with grand aspirations. As the deadline approached, the cement was hardly dry on the pad holding the satellite dish. A mere 36 hours before the House was scheduled to go on the air with a live feed, the technical side of creating a national network with the capability to uplink to a satellite was completed.

The operational side of the venture matched its technical side in terms of just-in-time functionality and shoestring capability. C-SPAN got on the air more because of grit and gumption than adhering to a master plan or marshalling significant resources. The 300-square-foot office studio—the size of a one-car garage—was so tiny that one of its denizens worked out of a closet. The office equipment consisted of a 30-year-old typewriter and a shaky table that you had to hold up with your knee. "Fly-by-night" would have been a charitable description. But somehow it worked.

C-SPAN went on the air with little fanfare March 19, 1979, with one slice of public affairs in Washington, gavel-to-gavel coverage of the House of Representatives. A technician threw the switch and the House of Representatives came on live. There was no lead in with the typical "coming up next." The initial bridge was pretty primitive, with its one-way transmission, single program comprising entirely of House of Representatives sessions, and limited audience. But it was a foothold gained by significant effort and great commitment.

A MODERN MULTIPURPOSE STRUCTURE

Twenty-five years later, Brian's one-lane bridge had turned into a massive three-lane structure, with multiples lanes of information. Brian's personal signature program, *Booknotes*, featuring the now-expected, far-ranging, one-hour interview with a single author, created a unique and vibrant bridge between readers and authors. It came as some surprise when the program went off the air in 2004. It had drawn some of the most important American authors, including ex-presidents of the United States. For fifteen years, Brian's Sunday evening in-depth interviews had been the staple of book lovers nationwide. Consistent with C-SPAN's different take on the media, Brian stayed in the background, asked probing questions, and let the author sink or swim on his or her own. Ever prepared, Brian spent 20 hours per week reading the entire book, making copious notes, and often surprising even the authors with his in-depth knowledge of their work. The effort of preparing for 800 interviews cost him 1.8 years of his life. The nature of the interviews varied little, from the first with Zbigniew Brzezinski, Jimmy Carter's National Security Advisor, on his book, *The Grand Failure: Birth and Death of Communism in the 20th Century*, to the last with Professor Mark Edmundson on his book, *Why Read*. Brian's unexpected, but quintessential Lamb question for Edmundson was, "Why read?"

It is tempting to see the two events as the beginning and the end of an amazing media ride, relegating Brian Lamb and C-SPAN to a historical oddity of bridges past. For Brian, though, they were simply markers along the way. As proud as he was of *Booknotes*, he recognized that no format or program is sacrosanct. He showed up at work the next day after the last *Booknotes* taping, ready to march forward. The bridge was not closed, just reconfigured. C-SPAN is more of an idea than a format. It is an idea that has deep roots in Brian's background, tempered by experiences far preceding even serious thoughts about the creation of a public affairs network.

If you have read this far, you are contradicting Brian Lamb's assumption. He asserted, "I cannot imagine anyone wanting to read about me. I really don't think I am very interesting. I am just too normal, and normality seldom sells." It is vintage Brian Lamb, modest, unassuming, yet frank. While some might pose and posture, puffing out their chest and telling an interviewer the momentous milestones in their lives, all the time wondering who would play them in the movie, Brian seems to show real concern for the interviewer that the project may be for naught. It is up to the reader to determine whether Brian is just an average guy; there remains little doubt that he has accomplished extraordinary things.

Bridges link *from* someplace *to* someplace and back again. In order to understand where Brian would go as a bridge builder, it is important to know where he came from. His bridges were ultimately designed to "serve the people back home," for whom he retained a great deal of respect.

2

THE FOUNDING FATHER
Building a Bridge on a Midwestern Foundation

As the twig is bent, the tree's inclined.

Alexander Pope (1688–1744)

Brian Patrick Lamb grew up in a "Leave it to Beaver" and "Father Knows Best" small-town setting. The two television programs actually dominated the airwaves (1957–1963 and 1954–1960, respectively) during Brian's early years. While today's references to the programs lean toward parodies, for Brian and his friends, the sitcoms of their childhood represented both reality and vivid representations of how things should be. Like the programs, life in Lafayette saw women serving as housewives taking care of the home. Discipline came from the threat, "Wait until your father gets home." At the time of Brian's 1941 birth and through much of his childhood, World War II still loomed in people's minds. Gold Star Mothers displayed their symbols of a fallen soldier in their windows and garnered the respect and sympathy of both friends and strangers. The Lamb's next-door neighbor bought a piece of land from them and followed the national unease about a nuclear war by building a bomb shelter. The above ground entrance, clearly visible from the Lamb home, served as a visual reminder that the world was filled with real threats. Good and bad stood out more clearly both in international and domestic affairs than the gray that would dominate in succeeding years. Illegal drugs were virtually unheard of and parental respect the norm. It was a naive, slower, and simpler life. Brian's childhood was happy if not particularly notable. His parent's instilled responsibility. Although not a stellar student, he never missed a day of school. As a child, his friends dubbed him "Doo," because of his resemblance to Howdy Doody, puppet star of the dominant children's program of his day.[1]

The Lamb roots lay in County Mayo, Ireland. His great grandfather, Terrance, emigrated in the 1860s. Bypassing the more common destinations of Boston or New York, he chose Delphi, Indiana, about twenty-five miles east of Lafayette. Favored by a local Republican politician, Terrance landed a job as church sexton at the local Catholic church, cementing the Lamb tie to the Republican Party and the Catholic church. Brian's Grandfather, Peter, could not wait to get out of Delphi and struck out for Lafayette and a career in the liquor business.[2]

Brian's parents, Bill and Opal, broke some of the norms of marrying within the clan. His mother, Opal Marshall, moved to Indiana from Arkansas. Her parents "were Church of God members and they weren't particularly fond of Catholics." The marriage challenged their conservative Church of God toleration of religious differences. Opal's mother felt that Opal's conversion to Catholicism, after meeting William J. Lamb, drove a wedge into the relationship between Opal and her parents. The linking of the Lamb and Marshall families resembled mixing oil and water. Bryan's grandparents on his mother's side opposed smoking, dancing, and drinking. Brian's father's long-term connection to the liquor business was probably also a source of estrangement. Whenever they came to the Lamb house, the liquor was hidden and the cigarettes remained unlit in the drawer. Bill Lamb did his best to affect a truce with his in-laws. They respected his business acumen and obvious love for their daughter. Opal's parents "softened their views over the years and became friendly to my father," Brian remembers.[3] Bill purchased a home for his in-laws, later on in their lives.

Brian grew up Catholic on Shawnee Circle, in a middle-class Lafayette neighborhood. He and his younger brother, Jim, regularly rose at 5:00 AM to serve weekday mass at St. Mary's Cathedral, and his father gave generously to the church. The Catholic church of the 1950s exuded tradition, with masses in Latin and the alter boys responding with memorized Latin responses. Religion remained important in Lafayette. Friends were labeled and described, largely without prejudice, based on their family's faith. Just after Brian entered the public high school, a Catholic high school opened, and he remained in one of the last classes forced to mix regardless of religion.

While we often think of discipline as externally motivated and enforced by punishment, true discipline comes from within. Years of Catholic school, 5:00 AM masses, and family examples left their imprint on Brian. He vividly remembers that at age 12, "right and wrong crystallized for me when I walked into a paint store and stole a simple paintbrush in Lafayette. . . . I walked down the street, got the most incredible guilt complex I'd ever had . . . marched right back and gave the paintbrush back."[4]

Opal Lamb exuded a quiet presence, but usually ran the family show. Jim, Brian's younger and more mischievous brother, remembers the night when a friend urged the 14-year-old to "borrow" the family car to pick him up. The friend assured him if they got caught, he would stand up for him. The caper went off without a hitch until they turned the corner and found Jim and Brian's parents home. Jim's friend began to sweat and backed out saying, "I was willing to stand up for you with the police, but not against your mother."

TWO TOWNS, ONE RIVER, FEW BRIDGES

Mention the word "Lafayette" and "Indiana" and most outsiders immediately conjure up an image of Purdue University, if they possess any image at all. Few, beyond the locals, realize that Purdue is located in the separate political entity of West Lafayette. Its residents are viewed as new political kids on the block by the denizens of Lafayette. The contemporary political and cultural domination of West Lafayette was not the case in Brian's early years. His hometown of Lafayette, across the Wabash River, was an old, blue-collar river town serving as a significant railroad hub and repair center with vibrant manufacturing plants for paper, liquor, and, later, prefabricated homes. Its residents were hardworking and hard-drinking, with more than their fair share of saloons. Lafayette's diversity of economic endeavors, if not racial composition, protected its residents from most economic fluctuations. Brian grew up in a community where economic insecurity was of little concern. Lafayette was essentially a small town in the 1950s with about close to 40,000 residents. It did not take a lot of effort to know most of its residents, and young Brian took every opportunity to do so.

MY BROTHER'S KEEPER?

The almost two-year difference between Brian and his younger brother, Jim, do little to explain their differences. As many of Brian's friends and teachers put it, "Brian was everything that Jim was not." While both tried to emulate their father's success, Jim turned to athletics, a boisterous demeanor, few visions beyond Lafayette, and a career following his father's footsteps in the beer business. Brian avoided athletic participation, maintained a quiet but respected presence, sought success outside of the family business, and found great appeal in the wider world.

Even as a young child, Brian was the brains and his brother was the brawn. In Jim's words, "Brian never stoked anything; he was always on the inside, behind the scenes organizing things." As a young child, Jim was often taken along on Brian's schemes, always as the junior partner. Brian convinced Jim to help him put on a puppet show for their mother's card club, with Brian handling the puppets and Jim the lights. Brian was a tough taskmaster, chastising his brother saying, "You can't run the lights." A memory that remains vivid over fifty years later. To make money, Brian took on the challenge of a *Chicago Daily News* newspaper route having few subscribers. He again lured Jim into helping. A bit of the glow of entrepreneurship faded as Jim rode down the street on his bicycle making deliveries and a gob of tobacco juice from a passing bus hit him in the face. He looked around thinking, "where is Brian?" For Brian the predawn delivery route not only would serve as his primary source of money for two years, but also would give him access to the newspaper he would read every morning before school. Both the newspaper habit and its early morning timing would stick with him.

While great debates and research endeavors have explored the relative importance of nature versus nurture in developing the personalities of children, the Lamb family provides an interesting case study. While sharing the same genes, Jim and Brian are extremely different. The competition between the brothers was clear. The impact of nurture seems to depend on who was doing the nurturing. Jim ended up a great deal like his father Bill, in occupation, interests, and demeanor. Brian is much more like his mother, Opal. Brian's college friends remember the Lamb house as "a retreat with an open beer tap"; Bill Lamb was "a man's man, loud, boisterous, and exuding warmth." Jim, Bill, and most of the gang would be sitting around drinking and watching sports. Brian was more likely to be in the kitchen with his "mannerly and gracious" mother.

Friends can't help comparing Jim and Brian, though not to the degree and public nature of the characterizations of Jimmy Carter's buffoonish brother Billy or references to Bill Clinton's brother Roger's time in jail. Nevertheless, Jim remained the local boy with a string of business and personal successes and shortcomings, well known and liked in the Lafayette area. Brian ventured out into the wider world securing his own set of accomplishments and false starts representing the "local boy makes good" characterization. Brian, in a gracious and older brotherly protective stance, cringes at comparisons arguing, "Jim is his own man, not someone to be compared with me." They remain committed to each other despite the differences.

A BRIDGE TO SOMEWHERE

Brian's childhood sounds idyllic. The community of Lafayette, Indiana, was small and friendly. Its 40,000 people, during Brian's childhood, reflected traditional norms, with employed fathers, homemaking mothers, and obedient children. He calls it "middle, middle west," and claims "nothing but fond memories of growing up."

Shawnee Circle, where the Lambs resided, was a pretty, idyllic neighborhood in which to grow up. The houses were comfortable and the location commanded respect. Recently, the uniqueness of the neighborhood landed it on the U.S. Interior Departments National Register of Historic Places as part of the Highland Park neighborhood. In the innocence of the 1950s in the Midwest, children were given pretty wide latitude to come and go where and when they wanted. The valley behind Brian's house was breeched by a bicycle bridge that became the natural meeting place for children on both sides of the ravine. Below the bridge, kids played sports. Brian was not a natural athlete, but took his turn.

Not wanting to totally eschew the expected tie to sports in basketball-smitten Indiana and in competition with a younger brother for whom sports came naturally, Brian found a way to create a bridge for which he suited for and comfortable with. He became the clubhouse boy for the local semi-pro baseball team and manager of high school sports teams the rest of the year. As clubhouse boy for the Class D minor league baseball team, the Lafayette Red Sox, Brian's job was to sit in the press box and run the scoreboard, a perk facilitated by his father's role as president of the local team. Not willing to let an opportunity go by, he sat next to Gordon Graham, Sports Editor at the *Journal and Courier*, peppering him with questions about reporting. The relationship between Brian and the cigar-smoking, hard-drinking Graham at least partially flowed from the fact that Graham was the "steadiest customer of his grandfather's place of business, Lamb's Tavern."[5] The media was no longer some disembodied voice coming over the airwaves or stark type on a page; it emerged in the form of a hard-working and hard-drinking acquaintance pursuing real-world journalism, not some abstract theory.

There were some divisions that hung over Brian's childhood. The conflicting cultures and concerns of Lafayette and West Lafayette largely played out as a "friendly, but not vicious rivalry." Aside from the natural sports rivalry between the high school teams, kids from West Lafayette referred to those from Lafayette as the "river rats," reflecting the area's blue-collar shipping connection. The professionals and academics associated with Purdue University in West Lafayette remained largely newcomers with external frames of reference. Brian probably had to get over the "son of a saloon keeper" label. Liquor was a very contentious issue, even with the repeal of prohibition a decade before Brian's birth. Those who publicly supported drinking remember the "hypocritical church types who supported prohibition in public, but had their own personal access to alcohol."

For these and other reasons, the bridge behind the Lamb house was not only a physical reality of his childhood, but became a symbolic tie to Brian's origins. He remembers that while "many parents forbade their kids to cross because it took us away from our secure environment. Precisely because of this, that bridge became my symbol of access to the larger world."[6]

RULER AND RULES

There was little doubt that Brian would attend St. Mary's Parochial Elementary School. His family's ties to the church were long and deep. St. Mary's reflected an era of strong Catholic education in which schools remained fully staffed by nuns in black habits. The era of lay teachers and contemporary dress codes remained well off in the future. Rules loomed paramount and teaching emphasized rote memorization. The Baltimore Catechism,[7] developed in the 1880s, reigned supreme. Moral beliefs were taught using a series of over four hundred questions and answers. The nuns counted on repetition and memorization to instill proper belief and action. For example:

> 189. Which are the two great commandments that contain the whole law of God?
>
> The two great commandments that contain the whole law of God are: first, Thou shalt love the Lord thy God with thy whole heart, and with thy whole soul, and with thy whole mind, and with thy whole strength; second, Thou shalt love thy neighbor as thyself.[8]

As teaching methods changed in light of educational research, the Baltimore Catechism lost favor by the 1960s and was phased out. For Brian, though, it had been a staple of his education.

VENTURING OUT

There is a temptation to imagine Brian locked in one of those flat "flyover states," isolated from the wider world. That would be a mistake. During elementary school, Brian's parents packed up the family for Fort Lauderdale, Florida, for three or four months each year. Brian and his brother would be enrolled in local schools. The difference between Brian and Jim remained in the new setting. One year, Jim convinced Brian to join him taking boxing lessons. After a few punches, Brian's lack of enjoyment of anything athletic shown through as he took off the gloves and began throwing them.

A 125-mile trip to Chicago to Franklin McCormick, star announcer on radio station WCFL, allowed Brian to put a face to the voice that he had so often listened to. While others collected baseball cards, Brian's "scalps" were the announcers whose voices overcame geography.

Brian's first trip to Washington, D.C. almost became his last. With an uncle in charge of the Eisenhower inaugural float committee and having access to the major events, the whole family took a sleeper train to Washington. At 11 years old, his excitement about seeing Dwight Eisenhower's inauguration reached its peak as the train pulled into Union Station. The trip resulted in more excitement than anyone would have imagined. Rather than a reception from a brass band or even a smiling relative, Uncle George rushed the Lamb entourage off the train saying, "There has been a terrible accident, let's get out of here." The family worked their way through the crowds covered with clouds of dust to the sound of screaming police sirens. When their train arrived in Union Station, train #173, the "Federal Express" from Boston had been having minor braking problems and was running behind schedule. After leaving Baltimore, the engineer realized he was driving a runaway train. They cleared track 16 in Union Station's multilevel set of tracks. Train #173 glided on the floor above the train with the Lamb family and crashed through the floor ahead of them into the baggage area. If the floor had not given way, the train would have ended up in the waiting area. Amazingly, only 78 people were injured, and the station was opened three days later, although the engine remained buried in the building for months.[9]

I'LL NOT DRINK TO THAT

Alcohol played an important part in Brian's life, not so much as a personal pleasure but as a source of family income. His grandfather was a bartender. "Old Pete" used to keep his clientele happy by dancing with a full glass of beer on his bald head. Brian remembers stories of what his grandfather had to do to keep the tavern going and feed is seven kids, "including gambling in the backroom and payoffs of politicians."[10] A lot of alcohol flowed around the Lamb home. In Brian's words, "God, too much."

Climbing the economic ladder, his father, known as "Big Bill," owned two taverns, Chesterfields and Lamb's Tap Room. He later became a wholesale beer distributor. Bill "the Beer Baron" Lamb ran his tavern and later his distributorship honestly, not necessarily the norm of the day. At the time, under "Indiana's [liquor] licensing system, [Brian's] father, and many others, were beholden to the political establishment. . . . Every time a new governor was elected, Democrat or Republican, the father had to 'keep on the guy's good side' . . . and contribute financially." Brian said "It made me sick."[11] In order to protect his business, Bill Lamb organized the Indian Tavern Owners Association to lobby for their interests. In that position, he "oversaw the disbursement of legal financial contributions to both political parties. He was in the business of buying political influence, and he didn't mind who knew about it."[12] Brian remembers watching his father constantly "crossing the palm of politicians on the left and right just to keep his distributor's license. . . . He worked his whole life to clean up the corrupt system."[13] The Lamb beer "dynasty" would have folded if Brian had been the only son. He had no interest in going into the business, his younger brother, Jim, picked up the slack and took over the enterprise. But, the legacy stopped there when Jim sold the distributorship and went into the building business.

It was hard to imagine a son more different than his father. Bill Lamb loved loud parties, followed sports (especially Purdue) with a passion, enjoyed being the outgoing "hail fellow, well met," basked in the rough and tumble of politics, and affected sartorial grandeur exemplified by his pink cashmere sport coat. Brian, on the other hand, had little time for parties, tolerated sports, prefered quiet conversations, watched politics from afar, and would not have been caught dead in a pink sport coat.

To some degree, like Alex Keaton of the 1980s sitcom *Family Ties*, Brian's personal rebellion against his past moved him in unexpected directions. Alex, played by Michael J. Fox, was the son of liberal hippies who became an archconservative. Brian's rejection was more selective. His grandfather distrusted banks, insisting on carrying all his money in his front, right pants pocket where he could count it and pass it out as sparingly as possible. Brian's father rebelled by playing the man of means, joining the country club, playing golf, and driving a new Cadillac. Brian bemoans the fact that "we are living in a world where people want more and more material things." Brian was embarrassed by the Cadillac and did not like to be picked up by his father. Brian's financial conservatism garnered both respect and made him the butt of jokes in later years. Brian also rejected the smoking and drinking, so much a part of his family's culture and economic well-being. The son of a small town, Brian gravitated to the big city and even after trying a second stint back "home," found it unsatisfying. It was a great place to be from, but he didn't want to live there.

Brian's first introduction to the intricacies of politics came from his father's beer distribution business. Both law and political tradition created a system of territorial protection. Licenses were distributed by political means. In order to maintain one's license to distribute in a particular area, the licensee was expected to make campaign contributions. As the process changed, removing territorial protection and allowing competition, Brian's father was caught in the middle and became frustrated. Brian remembers, "I watched my decent and generous father bemoan, 'I gave them $50,000 and they did not come through.' I recognized that I did not want to live that way."

A revulsion against corruption was only one of the lessons Brian would take from his close association with alcohol. One of Brian's father's bars sat across the street from the *Journal and Courier*, the local newspaper, so the watering hole became the center for swapping stories about politics. Brian spent a lot of time listening to political chatter. A few decades later, the bar room conversations reappeared as the roundtable discussion of journalists on C-SPAN's "Washington Journal."[14] On the personal level, perhaps proving the assertion that prohibition against behavior creates a "forbidden fruit" temptation, Brian never became much of a drinker. It was no great symbolic gesture, rather a recognition of its increasing danger with added years.[15]

GIVING VOICE TO TALENT

Arriving at Jefferson High School ("Jeff" to the locals), shorter than most of his classmates, and retaining some of his childhood chubbiness could have spelled a rough transition, but his "stylish dress, politeness, and wide-eyed enthusiasm endeared him to the older students, as well as his instructors."[16] Brian overcame his trepidation about going from a Catholic grade school to the public high school by finding ways to interact and fit it. Being accepted loomed large, as did his fear that he was not good or talented enough. He had little to fear. Brian jumped into extracurricular activities, if not academics. He played drums in the high school band, served as junior class president, participated in Hi-Y (a YMCA service organization), and was selected for Boy's State. He was a natural leader, not afraid to stand up and speak. He also played in a band called John King and the Kingsmen. King looked like Elvis and sang his songs. He spent short stints in others bands, but consistent with his personality, never created a band with his name on it. Brian played drums, but never adopted the long hair persona of the period.[17] As president of the Broncho Broadcasters, the radio club he founded at Jefferson, Brian got his first airtime. Members proudly wore a miniature microphone pin with a "BB" inscribed on it. While the name of the club was a corruption of "Bronco," there was nothing corrupt about Brian's interest and abilities. As a senior, his skills had improved enough to get him to the statewide radio announcing competition, losing to the winner by one point.[18]

Brian's personality, oratorical abilities, and managerial skills allowed him to compensate for other shortcomings. Being part of the school choir was a sought after position, offering status and the ability to travel. Choir director Dick Jaeger admits that "Brian was never a wonderful singer, but he was a natural talker and leader. He knew what to say and, more importantly, what not to say." Brian became the announcer for the choir. Jaeger knew he would not embarrass the school as the choir's front man. "He always looked like he was just scrubbed with a corn cob, well dressed, and immaculate." In an era where students were either respectful of authority or diffident, Brian Lamb stood out. He would take on his favorite teachers with logic and facts. As one teacher put it, "you could argue with Brian Lamb without getting angry. He could forcefully disagree without being disagreeable. He didn't always win, but he brought a new perspective into the decision process."

Brian was popular in high school. Unfailingly polite to his teachers, he retained just enough irreverence for the respect of his classmates. Joining them for a forbidden smoke behind the school helped make him part of the club.[19]

THE APPLE AND THE TREE

While in some ways Brian was very much like his father in terms of core values such as honesty and responsibility and natural leadership skills, in many ways, the apple fell pretty far from the tree. He had absolutely no interest in his father's beer business and was happy to have a father who would cut him a lot of slack. His childhood lacked for little. On the other hand, his father had grown up with almost nothing and wanted everything. The symbols of success loomed large in Bill Lamb's life. He was proud to show off his nice house and fancy car, while discussing his winters in Florida. Brian, on the other hand, grew up with a great deal and wanted little more, in terms of material things.

TUNING IN, BRIDGING OUT

Brian's fascination with radio began early. In the mornings and evenings, he would sit in the family living room listening to the old Victrola. At night, he would curl up next to a small Emerson radio, listening to baseball games and music. He became fascinated with the call letters of distant stations and found their locations on a road map from the local gas station. Radio and the prospect of becoming an entertainer enticed Brian. As a child of nine, his mother forbade him from going to bed with the radio on. Showing ingenuity, he set out to build a crystal set that took no electricity and could be listened to using an earpiece that would not alert his mother. A helpful clerk at an electronics store referred him to a back of issue of *Popular Mechanics* giving detailed directions. The effort was not all that surreptitious since the "little boy in shorts and sandals growing up in Lafayette, Indiana [he] would sit on his porch and build crystal radio sets, trying to pick up local signals."[20] As he remembers it, "It didn't cost anything. Just got a little crystal and a piece of plywood and put a little coil on it, and I had a little earplug. And so I would get in bed and listen to the local radio station. You could only get one radio station."[21] WASK, the local station that would later become so much a part of his life, came to life as soon as his mother left the room after kissing him goodnight. The crystal set whet his appetite for politics and introduced him to politicians such as Richard Nixon (first elected to the Senate in 1950), Dwight Eisenhower, and communist-hunter Senator Joseph McCarthy. Drifting off to sleep in Lafayette, Indiana, Brian still retained the naïve belief that almost all politicians were selfless public servants, and the few miscreants would get their comeuppance by a competitive media carrying out honest and objective journalism.

As a young boy, Brian used the radio as his bridge to the wider world. Nashville's WLAC introduced him to rhythm and blues music unavailable in the Lafayette environs. Not only was the music new, but even more amazing, the disk jockey announced in such a way that it was hard to tell if he was black or white. At the same time, the white boy from middle-America was tuning in his radio in Lafayette, another young boy, Skip Gates, was listening to he same music and announcer, placing it into his black experience in his Piedmont, West Virginia, home. Years later, Henry Louis Gates Jr. (Skip), chairman of the Afro-American Studies Department, and Brian Lamb, host of *Booknotes*, would share their common listening experience. Both remembered trying to determine whether the disc jockey was black or was affecting black intonation for effect. The image of cultural and linguistic cues floating through the air from Nashville falling indiscriminately on the ears of widely differing individuals suggests the immense power of a nationalized media. The bridge of radio had brought the two young boys closer together than if they had been restricted to their narrow worlds of ethnic and social isolation. In Brian's words, "our common listening joined two very different worlds."

Brian expanded his view of the world by stopping by Mrs. Henderson's house. He remembers that he "would go down the street . . . where she had one of those old radios, and they could dial in all over the world."[22] At home, Brian spent a lot of his time listening to the radio, especially WASK and WAZY. The announcers, in particular, fascinated him. He also turned his dial regularly to WBAA (as in the sheep sound), the station run by Purdue University students, reflecting the school's agricultural school tradition.

Radio fascinated Brian, offering him more control of timing and program choice. Television was in its infancy. The Lambs purchased their first television in 1952, a 13-inch black and white set. With one television, centrally located, Brian's choice of programming gave way to that of his parents. Most television watching involved the whole family gathered around for *The Milton Berle's Texaco Star Theater* or the *Ed Sullivan Show*. The one exception was Dick Clark's *American Bandstand*. Arriving home from school, with his father at work and mother preparing dinner, Brian could transport himself away from insular Lafayette and see the latest dances and what the "cool" kids wore in Philadelphia. The format and appeal would stick in his mind and later play an important part in his career path.

Brian's early experience as a television consumer showed little resemblance to contemporary consumption. Today's teenager, armed with a remote with access to dozens of channels narrowcasting unique programming in "living color," stood as unrealistic as the exploits of 1950s movie and television space explorer Flash Gordon. Today's grazing television channels, an activity particularly enjoyed by young men, would have required Brian to get off the couch, go to the television, and physically turn the dial. The effort resulted in relatively little value, since only three network options existed and their offerings varied little. The idea of channels dedicated to sports, shopping, music, or news probably never crossed his mind. Limited options meant that television created "shared islands of understanding," in which a broad range of individuals received similar information. Conversations in school and at work began with the reasonable question, "Did you see what Milton Berle did last night?" The limited options of the previous night's offerings became the grist for conversation.

Although television was on the rise, radio captured more of Brian's fascination. As his interest in radio matured, a young local businessman, Henry Rosenthal, was seeking a way to get out of the family clothing business and into radio. Rosenthal started working part time for WASK, the station he hoped to buy. The station would allow local teenagers to dance in a room outside the studio. Rosenthal noticed the Brian spent more time with his nose pressed against the studio window than dancing.

One of the advantages of a small town and low teacher salaries lay in seeing one's teachers moonlighting at other jobs. Gawking at his high school broadcasting teacher, Bill Fraser, working at WASK, Brian would mouth, "Can I come in?" or "Can I put the headsets on?"[23] As a neighbor, station owner Rosenthal knew Brian, so when he expressed interest in radio, a lifelong friendship was forged. Rosenthal gave Brian his first regular job, doing odd jobs around the station for $1.00 an hour. Brian would learn how to cue records and pull stories off the wire. Brian and Rosenthal were learning radio together. Rosenthal was less than enthralled with much of the station staff that he had inherited and was looking for new talent to enliven the station. One night as he was leaving, Rosenthal looked at Brian and said, "Why don't you do the station break at seven tonight?" It was a test for both of them. Petrified, Brian got through his debut on the air by saying, "WASK radio, 1450 on your dial, Lafayette, Indiana. Next up, Mutual News," a script he remembers over forty years later.[24] Brian was hardly off the air when Rosenthal's phone rang and Brian asked "How did it sound?" Brian was hooked on radio and had found a vehicle to express himself. Later, Rosenthal pulled him aside and told Brian he wanted him to do a 30-minute program that night. He was to choose the music and was told "I want you to record it, so you can have it for posterity, because some day it will mean something to you." His final piece of advice was, "Don't think a lot about this or you're going to be a nervous wreck."

Both Rosenthal and Brian used each other for mutual benefit. Rosenthal knew that Brian was very popular and "all the kids knew him." As one of his classmates put it, "Brian knew everyone in Lafayette. It was cross-generational. You couldn't drive anywhere in Lafayette with Brian without his waving to someone on each side of the street. He could have been the mayor of Lafayette. It was the same on campus. He would walk across campus and knew just about everyone."[25] In an attempt to get the station known, Rosenthal had a mobile station built in an old Volkswagen bus. Brian suggested taking it to Columbian Park, a popular hang out. Brian would spin records and the kids would dance in the street. It is "how he really found himself as a radio personality." His $1.00 per hour salary meant much less than the experience. All summer, Brian would drive out to the park and spin records from 7:00 to 9:00. Rosenthal's goal was more than filling airtime. As he explained to Brian, "Kids will come over, and we'll sell radio."[26] In the realm of "nothing new under the sun," over thirty years later, Brian came up with his own initiative involving a mobile studio build into an unlikely vehicle, to promote a broadcasting product.

Over the years, Rosenthal gave Brian a lot of leeway. He knew he had someone with talent and who knew most of the people in town. Brian would suggest taking the mobile unit to interview someone and Rosenthal simply would say, "Sure, kid." Brian probably gladly accepted the "kid" moniker since Rosenthal usually mangled his first name into "Bi-ron."[27]

It is hard to imagine Brian Lamb, the unflappable interviewer, as the pimply-faced 17-year-old who messed up his first big interview. His big catch for the little 240-watt station he worked for was the Kingston Trio. They were on the top of the charts and major stars. Brian set up his new Wollensak recorder in the renovated Volkswagen bus in the parking lot behind a music store in Monticello, Indiana. He reviewed the lessons from his high school broadcasting teacher—focus on who, what, why, where, when, and how. "Who are you? What do you do? Where do you come from? And why do you do this?"[28] The interview went well until Brian tied it up and said, "Gentlemen, if you don't mind, let me check my tape." To his horror, he realized that he had never pushed the "record" button. His heart sank. Screwing up his courage, he said, "Guys, this is everything to me. If I go back to Henry Rosenthal, it's over. It's just over."[29] He then asked, "Is there any way you guys would do it again?" Much to his relief and without missing a beat, they said "sure."[30] It was a good lesson in telling the truth.

Proximity to Purdue University provided opportunities to interview people like Duke Ellington, Count Basie, Bob Hope, Johnny Mathis, and Louis Armstrong performing at pre- and post-football programs called "Victory Varieties." The opportunity to do multiple performances on the same weekend on the same campus was both personally appealing and financially profitable for the entertainers. For Brian, working in radio was his access to anyone and everyone. The microphone served as his entrance ticket, while his personality and persistence served as his foot in the door.

One of Brian's first confrontations with mortality came through his radio programming. He had been producing live broadcasts of a very popular local musical group, the Fabulous Flame Brothers. One of the bothers died in a tragic automobile accident, and Brian rose above grief to "put together a radio tribute that would tear your guts out."[31]

Although somewhat shy, sitting behind the microphone emboldened Brian and helped him live up to the expectations of his father. Brian describes his father as "very curious" and a real "social butterfly." He was interested and involved in everything. He supported Brian's foray into radio and wanted to own a radio station himself. He always told his son, "I wanted to buy that radio station for you."[32] Brian wisely recognized that would have been a mistake, limiting him to being a big fish in a small pond.

LOCAL BOY STAYS LOCAL

The shift from Jeff High to Purdue University was smooth. Although he lived on campus, Brian was only a few miles from home. He even kept his job at the radio station. Brian looks back at the decision to go to Purdue as a mistake. Not that there was anything wrong with Purdue, rather the mistake was staying in his hometown. The $125 per semester tuition and the ability to maintain his ties to home looked appealing to someone not really ready for more education at that time. He admits to being a C student who "wasn't ready to learn."[33] He describes his educational endeavors as marked by memorizing and getting by "by the skin of my teeth."

As the hometown boy going to college, Brian had some advantages; a home nearby with an open beer tap and a convertible. One of his future fraternity brothers commented, "I saw this convertible coming down the street with something like twenty-five people hanging out of it and I thought, 'I've got to get to know this guy.'" As the fraternity rush began to wind down, Brian and a group of new friends decided to take control of the situation. They offered themselves up as a group to the brothers of Phi Gamma Delta, figuring that "we might as well pick the people we want to live with."

Brian's frustration with the lock the three networks had on the news emerged sitting around the fraternity house with a small cadre of news junkies. While others were doing their thing, Brian and his friends watched the news. Most of his fraternity brothers did not care about watching the news or reading news magazines and discussing them. One of the participants remembers Brian expressing the frustration that, "It is a shame we can only get the news from the three networks. Some day, I want to do something about it." Brian's success must be placed in the context of the thousands of hopes from college years that never reached fruition.

While his fraternity brothers ran around in tennis shoes or scuffed loafers, Brian was always impeccably dressed. His shoeshine kit was one of his key possessions.

Brian may have been different than most of his fraternity brothers, but he had their respect. Shortly before graduation, a group decided to break his perfect class attendance record that went back to his first day of elementary school. Locking him in his room in the fraternity house seemed like the perfect answer, but he was able to talk himself out.

Part of Brian's appeal lay in the fact that he was "Mr. Nice Guy." After a fraternity brother's wedding, Brian and another friend took off in their car chasing the bride and groom in order to find and decorate the honeymoon car. When the bride and groom jumped from the car to throw off the pursuers, Brian was tasked with chasing them through the shopping center and foiling the escape. In the midst of the chase, Brian saw a crowd of people around a child whose pant leg was caught in the escalator. Without a second thought, Brian stopped to help and let the honeymooners go on their way, much to the chagrin of his co-conspirators.

For most students, college represents both a physical and psychological break from the past. For Brian, it was little more than moving across the river and continuing his passion for broadcasting. As part of his efforts to expand his radio station's reach, Henry Rosenthal decided to take the station to the people, and loyal announcer Brian was there to help. He talked the largest department store in town, and one of his big advertisers, into hosting an onsite broadcast every Saturday morning. There was one hitch, Purdue had Saturday morning classes, and freshman Brian had a perfect attendance record all through school. The solution required a compromise. Rosenthal would arrive at Loeb's Department Store early to set up the equipment. Brian would get permission to leave class twenty minutes early, dash to the store, and immediately go on the air with Loeb staff and customers.

Brian got his start in television in 1961, while a junior at Purdue University, as a host of "Dance Date," fashioned after Dick Clark's *American Bandstand*, a staple of his television viewing in his younger years. He "built the sets, got the dancers, and went to advertisers."[34]

BRIDGING THE WIDER WORLD AND BRINGING IT BACK

In 1964, Brian and a fraternity brother traveled through Europe. Less interested in places than people, Brian sought out opportunities to get to know individuals. Brian's personality and style seemed to encourage people to open up. While staying in a private home in Amsterdam, dinner started with benign conversation when Brian asked them about what it had been like during the war. The hosts began a hushed conversation, punctuated with "should we tell them?" and out flowed an emotional story. One day, the wife came home to find eight or ten neighbors lined up against a wall, charged with harboring Jews in their house. With such summary justice, all were mowed down by the troops. Then everyone else was told that this was their last chance to save themselves if they had Jews hidden away. It was more than an academic question, since the wife knew they had a Jewish family in the attic. She nodded her head no and proceeded home. This was the first time she had talked about the experience to an outsider. Brian, the "skillful introvert," had shown an ability to extract information.

Although his official major was Speech, his forte remained making friends and getting involved. His route to becoming senior class president lay not so much in a long-term plan based on unbridled ambition, but more of an off-handed suggestion that he run and a poorly thought out "heck, why not?" response.[35] Known by almost everyone due to his outgoing personality and visibility on radio and television, he had little trouble winning the election. As senior class president, he would be giving the graduation speech. Although the Purdue administration had few fears of dealing with a rebel when the mature, classy, and understated Brian was elected president, he was not a "goody two shoes." The night before graduation, a group of friends threw him in a campus fountain after a night of celebrating. With the police on their heels, they tore off in an attempt to escape. Brian ended up jumping out of the car "and climbing like a Marine on all fours through the bushes" to escape. The speaker had not been busted.

The commencement speech proved predictable. No cries to "end the war" or "burn your bra" would float over the campus. He thanked the institution for the opportunities it provided and expressed the sweetest words any college administrator would want to hear, a remonstration to his classmates to provide "not only moral but financial support." The speech stands as a paean to well-considered individualism, decisiveness, imagination, and courage; character traits Brian would demonstrate throughout life. His quotes from philosopher John Stuart Mill, poet John Masefield, and journalist Henry

Grunwald stand the test of time. In the mode of Yogi Berra's "déjà vu all over again," Brian was asked to speak at the 2001 graduation of Ivy Tech, a community college associated with Purdue. On the same music hall stage he had mounted almost thirty years earlier, Brian faced the 6,000-seat auditorium and pulled out the same graduation speech he had prepared as a graduating senior. His penchant for saving everything paid off and the speech was a success.

A BRIDGE NOT SEEMINGLY TAKEN

Through his formal education, Brian did not seem to see education as an important bridge to broader understanding. He went through the motions politely and diligently, but lacked the passion to make the most of it. He explains his C average as just not being ready to learn.

For teachers, Brian may be seen as inspiration, not because of his stellar performance in the classroom, but to show that the C student in the back row is still absorbing attitudes, outlooks, and information that may prove fruitful in the future. Some students are just not ready to show their full potential. Brian credits his high school broadcasting teacher, Bill Fraser, with teaching him the art of interviewing, which is based on listening to the interview subject.[36] The importance of timing revealed itself in Brian's ability to take the broadcasting class. Only a year before, Fraser petitioned state authorities for permission, making Jefferson only the second school in the state with broadcast journalism. In college, Eric L. Clitheroe taught philosophy and religion both through content and by the way he lived his life. He showed great patience and served as an example of a great reader. Some of the lessons Brian learned lay dormant for decades, only to re-emerge when needed.[37] He explains that "where you place your efforts at one time in your life does not doom you to perpetually remain at that level of understanding and performance."

NUNSENSE

Brian's first independent foray into commercial entertainment occurred between graduation from Purdue and attending law school. With nothing to do for the summer, he decided to be a promoter. Finding that he could book rock and roller Bo Diddley, all he needed was a venue. As a product of Catholic education, he immediately thought of the local Central

Catholic High School. He booked it as a charity event and received the blessing of the nuns. Worried that Bo Diddley might live up to his reputation of showing up late or missing a gig altogether, Brian drove ninety miles to Michigan City the day before to confirm he would be there. Brian waited nervously as the minutes passed by, but true to his word, Bo Diddley arrived only forty-five minutes late and Brian felt he was out of the woods. Little did Brian know that Bo's sister had come along, wearing a tight fitting, silver lamé outfit. As she started to bump and grind, Brian thought, "I'm toast. It's over for me." Brian grabbed a local policeman, went back stage, pulled open the back curtain, and told the drummer, "Tell him [Diddley] to stop this now . . . I'm going to be finished." The concert went on without the suggestive dancing. They next day Brian went to the school to deliver the profits, about $100. The only feedback he received was from the secretary who said, "I understand the kids got quite an education last night."[38] Years later Brian saw Bo Diddley selling paintings on the streets of New Orleans. Remembering his nervous, but exciting evening with him, Brian bought a painting for $400. It sits in his office and "everybody who comes in says, who's that?"[39]

ILLEGAL TURN

Itching to get out of Lafayette and see the world, Brian's move ended in a misstep. Brian's law school foray was short and misguided. For once in his life, he let others tell him what to do. His father saw law as "a license to steal," and touted it as a great opportunity for his son. Others saw him as a "talker" who was a natural for the law. The governor was a neighbor, and his recommendation carried a lot of weight in a state school that did not require taking the LSAT (Law School Admissions Test). Admitted to Indiana University School of Law, Brian moved to Bloomington and was on his own for the first time. After three days of classes, he decided that he did not want to go to school anymore and didn't want to become a lawyer. Brian was still in the orientation session in Bloomington when his acceptance into the Navy arrived. Brian remembered a basic outlook repeated in his life: "when I am really on the wrong track, I literally get a knot in my stomach like I've never had since and knew that something was desperately wrong." From the experience, Brian followed his lifelong principle, "If you don't want to do what you are about to do, don't do it. Because if you don't believe in what you're going to do, you are not going to do it well and you're not going to be happy."[40] Cutting his losses, he quit law school.

Brian retreated to home ground, the studios of WASK radio and TV-18. It was the fall of 1963 and regrouping was the task at hand. He had just placed a record on the turntable and had a few minutes of freedom. As he got up to routinely check the wire service machine one late November afternoon, little did he know how much the world would change almost before he could sit down. Brian cut into the music to read the news bulletin of John Kennedy's assassination. Although neither the conservative community nor Brian personally were big supporters of Kennedy's policies, that did not make them immune from being deeply moved by his death. Brian remembers how dark the sky seemed as he drove home from work that night, almost reflecting the nation's darkness.[41] For the next thirty-six hours, Brian joined the nation as they watched the funeral and the shooting of alleged assassin Lee Harvey Oswald. Not wanting to watch alone, Brian alternated between his parent's house and returning to campus as a recent graduate to watch with his more junior fraternity brothers. Again the lock the three networks had on the news rankled him.

DEPARTING PORT LAFAYETTE

Although the Wabash River played a large part in the economic development of Lafayette, it served as little more than a line of demarcation between Lafayette and West Lafayette for Brian. He did not develop a love for the water cruising on the Wabash. Unlike many Midwesterners with little firsthand familiarity with the sea, fascination with the Navy did not come indirectly through comic strips such as *Don Winslow of the Navy* (also produced as a movie serial) and *Men of Annapolis* (1957). As would be his pattern throughout his life, personal experience played more of a role in his learning. Entering the Navy resulted less in a well-researched and rational positive choice than a small dose of negative experience in Army ROTC and his impression that around Purdue "the Navy ROTC participants just looked sharper." In 1963, with the Vietnam conflict growing and the draft looming, "you either picked your service, or it picked you." While he was active in Army ROTC at Purdue, Brian did not like it.[42] Facing a two-year obligation, he wanted to choose how it would be fulfilled. The Navy became his ticket out of town. Brian decided he could see more of the world with the Navy, and "it is a lot more comfortable than a foxhole somewhere."[43] Brian took the "Join the Navy and see the world" recruiting slogan to heart and readily admits, "It really worked out in my case." After twenty-two years in the same town and many of his friends anticipating spending the rest of their lives there, the decision to sail away from the anchors of family and community loomed large. Brian calls it "the most important decision in my life."

The first stop on his tour began with six months at Officer Candidate School (OCS) in Rhode Island. Assignment to the USS *Thuban* was less a reward than a booby prize. The longest U.S. navy ship in continuous service, the *Thuban* deserved its appellation as an "old, tired rust bucket." By the time Brian arrived on board, this warhorse of World War II, had been in service for over twenty years. Officer Candidate School officers helped make ship assignments after the first six weeks. Never a stellar student, Brian's standing at six weeks scraped the bottom of the class. By graduation, he had moved to the middle of the class, but the die had been cast. So off to the *Thuban* he went.

Officer Candidate School proved a life-changing experience for the kid from central Indiana. Awed by meeting his first admiral, he found himself shocked into the reality of his new commitment when Admiral King stated without any sugarcoating, "You're god-damned here to die for your country." The fantasies of spiffy uniforms and government-funded recreational cruising immediately evaporated.

Arriving to report to the *Thuban* from his stint at OCS and Amphibian School in Little River, Virginia, Brian carried with him the advice of a senior enlisted chief: (1) Don't show off your college degree, (2) Wear your uniform proudly, and (3) Don't ask for leave. When he picked up a rather cocky classmate from OCS to go to the ship, Brian was appalled to see him wearing a preppy civilian outfit with a fraternity pin as a tie tack, Brian thought, "We are not on the ship yet and he has already broken two of the rules." The third rule was shattered when almost the first words out of his friend's mouth to the division head was, "I have not had much time to spend time with my girlfriend, can I take some time off?" Brian remembers, "I almost fell off my chair." If the lesson that one needs to read the environment and learn how to comport oneself had not yet sunk in, a few weeks later, Brian and his friend responded to a loudspeaker for anyone wanting to see a giant sea bass. When the curious friend bent over to peer in the box, the navy chief swatted him with a paddle. It took him a while to recognize he had been the butt of a right of passage joke. The friend's denseness garnered him the nickname "Tackline," the six-foot vacant space between signal flags on a ship.

Onboard ship, Lamb quickly realized that he was a 22-year-old "punk kid" without a lot of experience either in the Navy or in the real world. He wore an officer's uniform, carried an ensign's rank, and merited a salute by enlisted subordinates who knew more and had experienced more than he ever would. He accepted the fact that the chief petty officer was the "heart and soul of the ship." Chief Petty Officer Hancock was "an old salt" who guided him through the paces. One of Brian's first responsibilities was as first division officer, making him responsible for the twenty-two men stationed from the ship's superstructure forward.

Life on the *Thuban* reinforced in Brian the importance of teamwork. For the first time, he realized that "unless you can work with others, you are toast." For the first time in his life, Brian had real responsibility, not only for himself, but for the life and property of others. The first time on the bridge steering the 13,000-ton *Thuban*, Brian faced a real challenge. The ship was underway in formation, a tricky endeavor under any condition, when they came upon a Russian trawler. Unfamiliar with what to do, Brian took little time to call down below, "captain to bridge." He felt great relief when the captain arrived to carry out the necessary maneuvers.

The *Thuban* was one and one-half football fields long and over sixty feet wide. Brian found both the new environment and new responsibilities as shocks, where "you are accountable to people that you didn't know . . . and you prove yourself every day. . . . You couldn't fall back on your father or mother or your friends in your hometown environment."[44] Although Brian has interacted with every president since Lyndon Johnson, he credits his petty officer on the *Thuban* with teaching him one of his key lessons in leadership.

As a freshly minted LTJG, Brian may not have mastered all the bookwork in OCS, but he did understand the key principles of human interaction. New "college boy" officers often arrive with a false sense of their own knowledge and capabilities, strutting around like peacocks, showing off their new status. Facing his men as an ensign, he quickly realized that "My petty officer fought in World War II. Relying on one's petty officer reduces the potential for making mistakes." Brian, petty officer by word and deed, imparted some key lessons, "When you don't know something, don't stand up and pontificate. True respect must be earned. Without respect, the crew will offer the trapping of false respect, but belittle you and pull the rug out from under you when can't see them. You don't come on and act like you know the world." He recognized early that one learns as much more from listening and observing as from talking and doing.[45]

Brian's experience onboard ship was an eye-opener for a young kid from the Midwest. He visited seventeen countries and "learned a lot about the world that I never would have learned had I stayed in Lafayette, Indiana, for the rest of my life." Continuing his role as a bridge maker and desiring to hone his reporting skills, Brian recorded audiotapes of his experiences and sent them back to his friends and parents. He "wanted the people back in my hometown to have the same experiences I had."

On the *Thuban*, he was thrown into an environment with over three hundred people having various backgrounds and interests. At 22, he was given significant duties, serving as officer of the deck (OD) of a vessel that would cost over $6 million to replace at that time.[46] As OD, one serves as the Captain's direct representative, having responsibility for the ship. Brian suspects that "not many people at that age get that kind of responsibility."[47]

Not all his tasks were as lofty. In his modest way, Brian remembers that most of the time, "I supervised the crew. We chipped paint and kept the area in shape."

With two years of his Navy commitment under his belt, the next step would be crucial as a bridge to the rest of his career. Before looking forward, it makes some sense to look backward to gain a short thumbnail sketch of where Brian Lamb had come from.

CREATING THE PACKAGE

Not all personal characteristics seamlessly emerge from early life experiences. While the politics he heard discussed at home had a strong Democratic Party accent, Brian has long eschewed affiliation with any political party. Perhaps his views came from the bifurcation of his "two" hometowns. The political ideology of Lafayette reflected Midwestern conservatism. Despite its blue-collar economic base, Lafayette voted "By God, Republican" until recent times, while West Lafayette, with its educational elite, was Democratic. Even the Democrats in Lafayette were conservative on most issues. Lafayette's conservatism was rooted in comfort with traditional ways of doing things both politically and socially. As Lafayette's town historian put it, "We are part of Indiana's unique stance; we have never done anything for the first time."

A late convert to voracious reading, Brian remembers, "My parents didn't read much at home."[48] Neither one of his parents was well educated, although both encouraged education. Threaded through his endeavors, lies a deep curiosity and a desire to learn that goes well beyond academic inquiry.

Brian remembers life in small-town Indiana as a setting where "nobody puts on airs, everyone was given a chance, and people supported you in everything you were trying to accomplish."[49] He reflects a basic decency, commitment to hard work, and respect for honesty. The lessons clearly sunk in, sounding like a good description of both Brian and the entity he would go on to found. His early friends say it well; few grasped for words to describe him, using a mix of colorful analogies and hackneyed (if correct) slogans:

> "They broke the mold when they created Brian."
> "Brian is like the ice cream store that only serves consistently high-quality vanilla ice cream. He allows the user to add the flavor."
> "A skillful referee who manages the game without being in the game."
> "Lots of people consider Brian their best friend."
> "A real steady-eddy you can count on."

3

A BRIDGE TO POWERDISE

Praise the bridge that carried you over.

—George Colman, the younger, *The Heir at Law*, Act 1

Individuals see the world through personal experiences that either challenge or reinforce one's information, attitudes, and behavior. Worldviews emerge from bridges to new realities embarked upon. Some people avoid new experiences and rely on comfortably reinforcing narrow perspectives, while others seek new options and revel in growing from them. Brian continually sought out new bridges to cross and willingly held his attitudes and outlooks up to the light of newly perceived realities.

The accumulation of experiences creates an idiosyncratic set of prisms, which in varying degrees, distort and/or clarify reality, helping one to interpret the world and define one's reaction to it. Some experiences create almost universal perceptions, across a broad range of individuals. September 11th certainly changed us as a world society, undermining some trust and hope. Virtually no one could avoid the bridge to the post-9/11 world, with its concern for security both psychologically and physically manifested in airport searches and coded levels of alert. On the individual level, being mugged leads most individuals to view the world as more dangerous, and undermines one's trust in others. Other experiences lead to more variable reactions. The defeat of one's favored political candidate could lead to political apathy and frustration with the "rigged political system," or it might reinvigorate one to redouble his or her efforts to "fight a better fight next time." Interpretations of competing experiences battle it out in our minds until one or the other prevails. Until we develop an equilibrium, the social psychologists tag us as having "cognitive dissonance," a fancy term for saying that all the fragments of our perceptions fail to fit together. Few of us are comfortable simultaneously holding diametrically opposed perceptions of reality. For example, we tend to view people as generally trustworthy or generally threatening. Once we have a firm perception of a class of events, we tend to seek out examples that reinforce our interpretation. People who distrust others create a growing litany of examples of human duplicity, either from their own experiences or those of others. It is not simply a matter of concepts in our minds. Seminal experiences, and one's interpretation of them, accumulate and guide future behavior.

At various points in our lives, we are more subject to perception-altering filters through which we view future events. Entering a new environment dramatically different from one's pervious experiences requires active management of one's perceptions. Periods of personal, organizational, and/or societal crisis, especially with the realization that past perceptions had led to personal or organizational failure, make the remolding of one's perceptual stained glass filter more likely. The arrival of Brian Lamb in Washington, D.C., in 1966, set the stage for a set of experiences that would mold the remainder of his life. It was probably the most important bridge he would ever cross. He was young (twenty-five), an advantage for remolding one's outlook. He was stepping into a set of national endeavors, one in Vietnam and another in the racially divided streets of America, both of which were increasingly difficult to frame as successes.

OPEN THE BRIDGE, HERE HE COMES

Countless individuals come to Washington, D.C. and have their lives changed—either for better or for worse. It is an alluring city filled with power lunches, sightings of the well-known, and numerous public events, each day, that appear on the evening news. One could spend virtually every day viewing a Supreme Court session, crowding into a Congressional hearing, or watching a demonstration. If one did not have to make a living, Washington is an excellent city in which to play the observer, watching the world of government and politics go by.

Washington is also a city that draws those enamored with power. The political power game is a fickle endeavor. Today's heroes, often instantaneously, turn into tomorrow's zeroes, at times by their own doing, and at others by changing events and public opinion. Washington's working denizens look for rising stars—both individuals and government programs—on which to hitch their aspirations. Some make lucky choices or work particularly hard and end up on the inside of the power game. In the process, they usually catch a full-blown case of Potomac fever, seeing Washington as the center of the universe and unable to imagine themselves working anyplace else. For most, entrance into the nation's capitol is a one-way bridge, where the return "toll" exudes the failure of being turned out. Arriving in Washington, Brian would clearly have his life changed by his immersion into the Washington power game.

The uniqueness of Brian's experience in Washington lies on both sides of the influence equation. He would not only be changed by Washington, but would, in turn, change the city and how it worked. It was not a grand plan, but rather an accumulation of experiences and reactions that changed Brian from simply one of those people who passed through Washington to one who left something significant in his wake. The uniqueness is enhanced by the fact that he accomplished it without following the normal path of appointment or election to high office.

CHARTING A COURSE

Brian's tour in Washington, D.C., was less an intended destination than a vehicle to practice skills that he enjoyed and thought would be marketable after his time in the Navy. Some naval officers bob in the water, accepting assignments chosen by their detailer (the naval officer charged with filling openings in a particular career specialty). Other officers do all in their power to guide their own careers, looking for openings and positioning themselves for preferred assignments. Brian readily took the advice of one of his friends that "One thing I've noticed about the military . . . is that the squeaky wheel gets the oil. If you want something . . . let the brass know."[1] When Brian's detailer indicated he would be spending his last year and a half on a ship rather than as a PAO (public affairs officer), he got in his car and drove to Washington to see if the CHINFO (Chief of Naval Information) office would request him and circumvent his detailer. The Navy Captain he talked to promised to try. Even after a negative response, Brian persevered. He called the Captain at CHINFO and asked, "What do I need to do to become a PAO?" The Captain said, "Extend your commitment for an additional six months." That sounded like a pretty good deal, and Brian found himself on the way to the Pentagon.

The first step into this new world meant going home. The Pentagon Press Information Training School was located in Indianapolis, Indiana, only about an hour from his Lafayette birthplace. While pleasant to be around friends and family, he focused his efforts on becoming a PAO. He remembers the pleasant surprise of hearing the mantra that Pentagon press officers should strive for maximum information with minimum delay. Leaving with such optimistic marching orders undoubtedly set Brian up for the frustration he would later feel.

Brian arrived at the Pentagon assigned to the audiovisuals division of CHINFO. All of his colleagues in the office were Navy careerists and liked their positions. After one month, when the call came in for someone to move to the audiovisual office of the assistant secretary of defense for public affairs, everyone looked at Brian. While the move might be seen as a big promotion, they viewed Brian as the most dispensable. He became a desk officer, answering phone calls from the networks and coordinating media events. While Brian would argue that he "never had an important job in the Navy," decisions he made determined what and when the media could access firsthand information.

A BROKEN BRIDGE

Moving from the audiovisual office, Brian served as Secretary of Defense "Robert MacNamara's spin doctor during the year the first troops landed in Vietnam."[2] The lieutenant's first job in the Navy's CHINFO Office involved going to Union Station at 5:00 AM every morning to pick up the daily newspapers, clipping the important stories, and briefing the CNO (Chief of Naval Operations) and a retinue of other admirals. He became the gatekeeper of their understanding of media reaction to world events. Knowing a chain is only as strong as its weakest link, Brian worked hard not to be that link. He admits being "scared to death," facing captains and admirals well beyond his pay grade, but it taught him to be a quick study who could cut to the chase and summarize complex material in almost real time.

It was a momentous time with "everyone's nerve endings highly tuned," as U.S. troops first landed in Vietnam despite Lyndon Johnson's 1964 campaign promise that he would not send American boys to fight on Asian soil. Brian remembers arriving at the Pentagon with few political views and "as a young, 25-year-old Midwesterner having my eyes opened to the world." As a public affairs officer, he spent all day answering the phone from network bureau chiefs asking about upcoming briefings or verification of events being reported out of Vietnam. Most of Brian's initial answers were "I'll find out about it."

Naturally open and accommodating, Brian eventually realized his unwitting role in spreading misinformation from the Pentagon. One of his tasks involved giving the Thursday afternoon weekly body counts to the press. Brian earned the unwelcome nickname of the "voice of the war god" from his friends.[3] Brian recalls, "I was only able to give the answers I was given. If they would ask, 'How many planes were lost in Vietnam?' [Pentagon officials] would say 5,000, when there were actually 10,000. . . . The same thing would happen with [soldiers] missing in action or killed in action. The figures would be delayed for days and days on purpose . . . so they would play in the news in a political way that wouldn't damage the president of the United States."[4] Brian would watch Defense Secretary Robert MacNamara's weekly press briefing with increasing dissatisfaction. McNamara would answer questions on the condition that they were attributed only to "U.S. officials," even though every reporter around the table knew exactly where they were coming from. Ever charitable, Brian says, "It seemed to me to be a fraud. I know the people involved in it then thought they were doing honorable work, and no one was per se lying at a particular meeting, although the Secretary didn't tell the truth all the time. . . . I kept saying to myself, there's something wrong here . . . the more insular it is, the more both sides can fool the public for their own reasons."[5] Brian soon began to realize that despite his public affairs training, the Pentagon practiced "minimum disclosure with maximum delay."

Brian's recognition of Pentagon duplicity developed slowly. The mixed messages made black and white judgments difficult. Brian saw himself as "committed to doing my job as a Navy person. I didn't have a political commitment. . . . In the early days, we didn't know that the Secretary of Defense was lying, but we found out as time went by because we had to put out press releases that weren't really true."

While MacNamara's approach was a more subtle form of misleading the media, others around Brian followed an even more nefarious path. Arthur Sylvester, assistant secretary of defense for public affairs, flatly asserted the government's right to lie.[6] While Brian could conceive of some rare situations where that might be the case, the breadth of Sylvester's claim bothered him. Brian could only conceive of narrow situations with grave consequences where that might be legitimate.[7] Brian increasingly sided with the "government in sunshine" movement, buying the assertion that openness serves as a disinfectant that drives out unwise and improper behavior. He developed a deep distrust of anything secret.

DEFENSES BEYOND THE BELTWAY

Being at the right place at the right time has given Brian experiences difficult to arrange or plan. His contribution lay in making the most of them. During the July 1967 race riots in Detroit, Brian received a summons to meet with one of the deputy assistant secretaries of defense. He was told, "Go home and pack your bags and take this tape recorder with you and fly to Detroit and report to the chief of police's office."[8] A domestic riot was in full flower. His record as a skilled briefer paid off, as he was tasked to serve as the eyes and ears of the White House and Department of Defense during the tumultuous race riots and Vietnam War protests. His job involved recording every press conference with then-Governor George Romney and transmitting it back to President Johnson both electronically and in hard copy. Despite serving in the Pentagon during the height of the Vietnam War, this was a new experience. Here in mid-America, there were tanks on the street corners and armed people in fatigues all over the place. Reporting for duty in a small room, Brian found himself surrounded by Cyrus Vance, deputy secretary of defense; Warren Christopher, deputy attorney general; John Doar, assistant attorney general; Dan Henkin, deputy secretary of defense; and Roger Wilkins, top civil rights officer in the Justice Department.[9] It was heady company, surrounded by the key newsmakers of the day. What Brian saw today would be on the front pages tomorrow.[10]

Despite long hours and a hectic work schedule, Brian's time in Washington allowed him to build his own personal Rolodex of whom he would call on and work with in the future. He and fellow naval officer John Evans dated roommates, and began a friendship that would have personal and business ramifications for the rest of their careers.

OBSERVATIONS OUT THE WINDOW

From his window in the Pentagon, Brian could watch the demonstrators "performing" with activity and violence only when the cameras were around, guaranteeing them a place on the evening news. On weekends, Brian would put on his grubbies and mingle with the Vietnam protesters on the Washington Mall. He wanted to decide for himself whether they were determined and bitter, or just there to have a good time.

SEEING IS DISBELIEVING

Public affairs staff served as project officers taking care of the media at particular events. Late in his time at the Pentagon, Brian was sent to monitor one of the war protests that had become almost daily affairs on the Pentagon steps. This day, his frustration was aimed more at the media than at the demonstrators or the Pentagon news managers. The assignment to facilitate media coverage of a group of lounging demonstrators who had been allowed to spend the night in front of the Situation Room by Secretary of Defense Robert MacNamara taught Brian an important lesson. The kids had walked all the way down from Bolinton, Connecticut. The scene changed dramatically as a camera began to roll. The kids got up, the placards came out, and they began yelling and screaming, "Stop the war. Stop the war."[11] One reporter, Bill Downs, was doing a "stand up," explaining the event with the demonstrators in the background. Downs, "a big, hard drinking, ABC television correspondent of the old school," was having difficulty getting his lines out. As if by "unspoken agreement between the demonstrators and the news crew—the lying-down-and-jumping-up routine repeated itself with each take."[12] All in all, it took seventeen takes. Brian's anger grew with each repetition, and he became particularly angry that all three networks were covering the same "story." In Brian's observation, "they had never screamed or shouted on their own. They had come peacefully. Nice kids."[13] At a minimum, Brian felt that "we ought to see the whole thing."[14] He realized that the story on the evening news would look very little like what he had observed in person.

COOL AIDE

Young officers with few outside commitments in Washington often commit their free time to sports or the bar scene, neither of which held much appeal for Brian. Washington can be a lonely place, and Brian's duties at the Pentagon failed to fill up all his time. Single and searching around for something to do, a friend alerted him to the need for military aides to work events at the White House. Brian set up an appointment with Bess Abell, President Johnson's social secretary, and was chosen as one of the twenty-five aides.[15] He was among four young officers who would prove their mettle in years to come: Alan Mertle, president of George Mason University;

Edward Mathias, cofounder of Washington's premier investment group; and Chuck Robb, senator from Virginia and son-in-law of President Johnson.[16]

While most officers left the Pentagon at night and quickly shucked their uniforms, Brian got out of the business suit he wore in the office and donned the uniform for official events. Perhaps because of his radio voice, it soon became his job to announce guests when they arrived for state dinners. Brian stood in the receiving line next to President Johnson, secured the guest's name as the guest moved toward Johnson, and I would turn to the president and say the name and he would say, "Well, hi, Bruce. Nice to meet you."[17] Since the most magical music to one's ear is his or her own name, it was critical that the president repeat it.

Hanging around the White House served as a graduate course in human behavior. Brian found that "even very big people are overwhelmed at being in the presence of a president. People would get captivated" when talking to President Johnson at White House events, remembers Brian, and not know how to end the conversation. "Our job was to keep the line moving."[18] Not all the experiences were positive. Brian remembers, "I was told off by Joan Crawford. She was not a friendly human being." White House guests treated the aides "almost like servants." He still remembers, "Barbara Walters treated me with disdain."[19] Early in his White House tenure, "Johnson paid no attention to me. He didn't even know my name. I was just part of the wallpaper." As Johnson's poll numbers began to drop, he took new interest, seeking out Brian to shake his hand and thank him. Brian says, "It was like he was reaching out for support to everyone he could and I was there."[20] On balance, the observation of Lyndon Johnson up close would lead to the conclusion that "Lyndon Johnson was a miserable human being. He treated people like dirt."[21] At best, he was just "less naturally gracious." On the other hand, Brian remembers Mrs. Johnson as "one of my favorite people whom I've ever met in public office because she was so decent to everybody." Despite the personal judgment, Brian experienced the awe of the office. Individuals ready to tell a president off often turn into meek sycophants in the presence of the leader of the free world. In Brian's words, it is "something you just couldn't get over, no matter who the individual was serving in the office."[22]

The White House experience helped prepare Brian for the potentially heady experience of interviewing presidents and other political leaders. The military requirement of being at ease in any situation soon became a learned reaction. Brian recalls that rubbing shoulders with White House guests took "the awe away from being around famous and important people. I was 24 when I first went to the White House. You're young and impressionable and overwhelmed by big names, but then you realize they're just people."[23] Brian's involvement in the political stratosphere increased when his fellow White House aide, Chuck Robb, became engaged to Lynda Johnson. Recognizing the extensive interest in a sitting president's daughter being married, Brian offered to be Robb's public relations officer. In preparation for his meeting with the press, Brian recorded a Q&A session with Robb. When it came time for the bachelor party, Brian edited the answers together with far wilder questions and ran the sound along with a film of President Johnson at a press conference. Robb remembers that it was done "in such a way that everybody howled."[24] Robb certainly was pleased at the good-hearted attempt to embarrass him in front of his future father-in-law and asked Brian to escort the mother of the bride at the wedding.

While wedding bells and happy faces would reign at the wedding, not everything was calm and pleasant. Lyndon Johnson, the ultimate news freak with three television sets installed in the Oval Office, happened to catch a news report mentioning that his son-in-law had a press secretary. Johnson went ballistic and called Brian's bosses at the Pentagon. In the president's mind, only one person in the White House was important enough to have a press secretary, and it was definitely not a certain junior-level military aide. By the time Johnson was done, Brian had been reassigned to desk duty. In his typical laid-back approach, he took the situation less as an offense and more as an opportunity, remembering that "being that close to controversy was very interesting to watch."[25]

Despite the flap, Brian played an important role in the wedding, escorting Mrs. Johnson into the ceremony and President and Mrs. Johnson out. Brian was the first one the Johnsons commented to about how well the wedding turned out. At the reception, he introduced all five hundred guests to the wedding party, a task taking nearly three hours. Senator Everett Dirksen (R–IL), one of the few Republicans to make the invitation cut, gave Brian a hard time in jest, asking in his unmistakable gravely voice to be introduced as "Calvin Coolidge," until his wife kyboshed the joke.[26] The benefit of the high visibility duty in the White House reverberated back home. When Brian went back to Indiana, he found that "the only thing I was known to have done in my life was to escort Mrs. Johnson down the aisle."[27]

Tailing the president of the United States was an extraordinary experience. Brian got to listen to conversations between the president and Secretary of Defense Robert MacNamara, Supreme Court justices, and other notable visitors. At one point, Brian's job was to take Supreme Court

Justice William O. Douglas to the bathroom, a task bound to take any luminary off his pedestal. After two years of this, "the awe that you might have about famous people was gone."

In the beginning, Brian was pretty naive about how the political system worked. Without cynicism, he is quick to point out that if you want to understand politics in Washington, you need to "follow the money." He admits that, "I've learned along the way the incredible importance of money in the system. Believe it or not, 20 years ago, I didn't realize that it was everything."[28]

STOKING THE FIRE

Ever curious and either brave or naive, depending on one's perspective, Brian sought out a full tapestry of experiences in the nation's capitol, eschewing the typical tourist destinations and finding its real politics and culture. In an era when many turned to illegal drugs, Brian sought his highs from directly experiencing events avoided by most. In 1966, Brian pulled on his jeans and grabbed his backpack of youthful curiosity. His venture took him into the relatively isolated Washington Black community to a Baptist church, where fiery civil rights leader Stokely Carmichael held forth. His was almost the lone white face in a sea of Negroes listening intently to the powerful speaker at a time before "African American" or "black" became the politically correct terms of reference. Those around him probably wondered why he was there as much as he did. For some, the experience might be seen as one of race or rhetoric, but he perceived it as a lesson in media strategy that would serve as a bedrock principle that would illuminate his view of reality and activate the remainder of his life.

CLASSIC CARMICHAEL

Although a transcript of the Carmichael speech listened to by Brian is lost to history, other transcripts reveals common themes and phrases. Undoubtedly, many of these words and themes wafted through the church where Brian was sitting. As the following excerpts indicate, Carmichael clearly spoke in frank terms to a black audience with a mix of political philosophy, facts, and emotional screeds. He said things that other black leaders only thought about, of which most white citizens wallowed in denial or ignorance.

- Frustrated with the white press corps and defining his audience, Carmichael expressed his frustration, saying: "So when the honkies talk tomorrow about violence and anti-White hating . . . tell them they ought to have a black man reporting it, cause they don't understand. Cause we talking to black folk anyhow."

- As the first to use the term "Black Power," Carmichael attempted to temper the fear of violence it created by asserting: "Black Power is the coming together of Black people to fight for their liberation by any means necessary. . . . . But the problem isn't one of violence, see. The problem is one of hitting back White people when they hit you. . . . So don't get caught up in no discussion about violence. We just making it crystal clear to the honky today that if he try to sheet us, we gonna kill him fore God get the news."

- Rejecting traditional solutions, Carmichael took on conventional wisdom, arguing: "The next lie they tell us is this about education. If you go to school and get a degree, you gonna make it, you know. All our college students, when they get out of college with a college degree, make less money than a honky with a high school degree."

- Linking his strategy with the Vietnam conflict that was garnering much of the public's attention, Carmichael set out his call to action: "You have got to understand that the war in Vietnam is calculated to get rid of us. . . . Our guts and blood have been spilled for this country and we go to the worst schools this country can produce. . . . Our guts and blood have been spilled for this country, its time we spill them for our people."

Source: Excerpts from Carmichael's April 19, 1967 speech in Seattle, Washington. Available at: http://courses.washington.edu/spcmu/carmichael/.

Brian tried to absorb the entire event while remaining as inconspicuous as possible. The incongruity of his presence did not seem to bother him. He remembers a reasoned and intelligent thirty-minute speech, capped by a couple of minutes of extreme rhetoric at the end. In his words, "Of a thirty-minute speech, probably, and maybe two minutes was incendiary. The rest of it was thoughtful and intelligent and very well stated."[29] When Brian turned on NBC's David Brinkley, he found it hard to believe it was the same event. As Brian remembers, "What made it on [the evening news] was the fire and brimstone. . . . It seems to me we were being unfairly treated as a society by the television news."[30] It became one more data point in Brian's disgust with sound-bite journalism controlled by a limited number of networks, resulting in misrepresentation of reality. As Brian remembers, "The experience of going there and seeing the whole speech did not mean that the pithy comments were any less important. It just meant that this man had more balance in his presentation by far than what you heard on the evening news. Years later, CBS journalist Daniel Schor admitted how he and his colleagues were in cahoots with the demonstrators in order to get on the air and to get paid more. The journalists would egg on the demonstrators and then pick the most incendiary comments." Perhaps it was a personal quirk or the Midwestern expansion of Missouri's "show me state" mantra that led Brian to conclude that such misrepresentation is the norm.

Brian moved from the naive question of "Are the media biased?" to the more sophisticated question of "How are the media biased, and what is the consequent effect on our interests and values?"[31] He was not quite ready to ask the question, "What can I do about it?" Brian explains that since that time, "I've always had a strong need to see things for myself, and I figured other people felt the same need."[32] This and similar experiences serve as the seed for the development of a new kind of television designed to give viewers access to as much of the full event as possible.

GETTING OVER BEING FROM A FLYOVER STATE

Being a Midwesterner in Washington is a challenge. Early on, Brian realized that "there is an enormous number of people that think [the Midwest] is flyover country. . . . There is an East Coast bias based on lots of very bright people who went to Harvard, Princeton, Yale. You walk into town, having been a Purdue graduate, and the first thing they think is that you are from a school 'out there somewhere.'"[33]

ANCHORS AWAY

Life in Washington can be exhilarating, but wearing. With his Navy career coming to an end, Brian had to think about the future. He wanted to stay in Washington, but was somewhat intimidated by those with whom he would have to compete. He started his job hunt in Washington with an interview with Senator Birch Bayh from his home state, but that did not lead to a job offer. His attempt to get a job in the 1968 Nixon campaign as a "personal valet," almost was consummated, but eventually "didn't work out."[34]

YOU CAN'T GO HOME

With few prospects in Washington and with greasing the skids by his father, Brian returned as assistant station manager to the television station where he had worked prior to joining the Navy. Although the new station manager did not know Brian, he had known the family for years. After an informal meeting at the Purdue–Ohio State football game, he offered Brian the $1,000-per-month position. It was not a marriage made in heaven. While Brian and the station manager remained good friends, the realization that television was, at its base, a business where one must program for what the audience wants, not what they need, left Brian cold. He was going to have to sell programming that he did not believe in. On the personal side, there was also no marriage in sight. His engagement had turned into an unengagement, and Brian needed some space.[35] Then an opportunity arose to become part of the media without being of the media.

Giving action to words, Kevin Phillips, the Republican activist, fulfilled the party's growing mistrust of the media by creating *The Media Report*, a watchdog publication designed to inform the Washington journalistic community and keep it honest. Brian became editor and eventually owner of a publication with a miniscule but influential audience. The experience focused his thoughts on the media industry and gave him the opportunity to refine his views on the principles of journalism he would later put into practice. While satisfying, the income from *The Media Report* failed to meet his modest needs. His former boss from Lafayette, Dick Shively, offered him a part-time job working for his cable system. For a year, Brian became a long-distance commuter, spending two weeks in Washington and two weeks in Lafayette every month.

Brian had never really lost his ties to Middle America. He recognized that his unique experiences had given him the opportunity to see politics in Washington up close and bemoaned the fact that the folks back home were never privy to much of what really happened. He harbored little desire to return to a small town, but wanted to make sure his friends and previous neighbors were in the information loop that would allow them to understand what occurred in Washington. When a chance to get back on the national scene appeared, he jumped on it.

Brian asked for a leave of absence to take a low-level job in the Nixon campaign. It was less a reflection of passionate commitment to Nixon than a socially acceptable ticket out of town. Ultimately, the draw of Washington would prove too great, as Potomac fever grasped another victim.

THE MIKE IS OFF

As Brian drove his red, 1963 Corvair into Alexandria, Virginia, in August 1968, he probably never realized how permanent the move would be. Recognizing Washington as a town where who you know can be as important as what you know, Brian went to Senator Howard Baker (R-TN), an acquaintance from his time as a White House social aide. Baker referred him to the right people who gave him the choice of two jobs. The most appealing paid $400 a month and involved travel around Michigan, Minnesota, and Wisconsin to take the pulse of Middle America in a program called "Speak to Nixon-Agnew." He was assured that an aide boiled down the tapes and shipped the results to Nixon and Agnew.

Brian could be naive if well-intentioned. About halfway through his two-month stint, Brian realized, "There is no way they're listening—there were 24 of us out there."[36] Brian later admitted that "it was all hooey, a gimmick to attract the attention of the evening news and plant firmly in the minds of the public that Nixon-Agnew wanted to listen to the people, but I really thought it was real."[37] After five weeks of the fraudulent charade, Brian put his foot down. He would no longer participate "because it just was not honest." Rather than fire him, the campaign staff allowed him to create his own programming. He would interview people about their reaction to the campaign and provide the answers to the press. Brian's skill, enthusiasm, and ethical standards had won.

Few experiences in life have no value. Rather than going away a disappointed cynic, Brian filed away the experience and looked for a way such an interaction between the public and public officials could be accomplished more legitimately.

BITING BACK

Brian's dream that working a few months on the presidential campaign staff would serve as his key back into the White House failed to materialize. Positions on the staff of Herb Klein, Nixon's director of communications, went to longer term Nixon loyalists, not to newcomers who questioned their methods. It was back to the streets again.

Perhaps out of a "if you can't beat them, join them" strategy, Brian began courting job opportunities in the media. After visiting seventeen countries in the Navy and experiencing Washington politics up close, Brian simply "wanted the people back in my hometown of Lafayette, Indiana, to have the same experiences I had."

Applications to the three network bureau chiefs also proved fruitless, although there was a lesson to be learned. In Washington, one gets labeled quickly. By working for the Nixon campaign, even in a lowly technical job, people had categorized Brian as a Republican. Brian only remembers seeing the president once, while passing in the hall. Bill Monroe, CBS Washington bureau chief, frankly admitted, "Most of the people around here are Democrats; I would love to have a Republican if I had the room." It is a lesson that Brian would have reinforced in the future.

Brian jumped on an offer from John Chambers seeking to add a second reporter to the Washington bureau of UPI radio. Chambers obviously overlooked Brian's last job or missed the irony of hiring someone from the Nixon campaign working for the son of Whitaker Chambers, one of Richard Nixon's key targets in his anti-Communism adventures of the 1950s.

The job in Brian's first love, radio, served as his introduction to the real world of big-time editing and sound bites. His job was to cover a news conference or hearing that might last a number of hours and to pull out the forty-five seconds that would be fed to radio stations. Brian developed a deep discomfort with serving as such a powerful gatekeeper of the news. The idea of sound bites still seems to leave a sour taste in his mouth. For the next few months, he survived on a pitifully low salary, but gained a new insight into how programming could be syndicated to a large number of stations at low cost for each.

TIME ON THE HILL

Chambers received an offer to serve as press secretary to Senator Peter Dominick (R-CO). Turning down the offer, Chambers recommended Brian Lamb, who took the job. Senator Dominick could not stand Vice President Spiro Agnew and wanted to replace him. The task required national publicity. Brian jumped into the task, contacting a friend on the *Today Show* who agreed to the booking.

Brian walked into his first day on the job with the *Today Show* coup impressing the senator. His staff, on the other hand, tried to block the appearance. They knew of Dominick's medical problems requiring hospital admission the next day, but never bothered to share the information with their new staff colleague. The Senator overruled the staff, which probably did not endear Brian to them. The *Today Show* appearance went well, but Dominick went directly to the hospital, where he spent the next six weeks. The second day on the job, both the senator and his staff wanted Brian to tell the press that Dominick was in for a routine checkup. Brian remembers thinking, "This is crazy, I didn't get into this job to lie for politicians." He knew that such a story was both a lie and would not work, a lesson seared into his being by his Pentagon experience. Thus, Brian told the press what was wrong and the press backed off.

One of the press secretaries Brian interacted with most was Paul Weyrich, who worked in the counterpart senatorial office of Gordon Allott (R-CO). Weyrich remembers his great relief at Brian's arrival, since his predecessor had been "unpleasant, uncooperative and, in my view, incompetent." Brian, on the other hand, was "such a nice guy . . . so easy to work with . . . [and] very competent."[38]

Life as a press secretary in the Senate emerged as a mixed experience. Brian found the Senate to be "an adoring atmosphere with everyone catering to his or her big man." On the positive side, he was earning $16,000 a year and "on the inside looking out." Placing himself in his typical learning mode, Brian absorbed the new experiences. Contrary to Count Otto Von Bismarck's advice that there are two things one should never see made, sausage and legislation, Brian took advantage of the situation. He remembers, "All these were good experiences. I had been in the sausage room and saw how much was covered up." The experience would reinforce his feeling that too much around Washington was done in secret.

As press secretary to Peter Dominick (R-CO), Brian soon learned the ability to gain media attention stemmed not from reasoned arguments or insightful choice of issues. He found that "if you didn't say almost irresponsible things you never got heard. You had to accuse, or 'view with alarm,' or attack."[39] Especially in the electronic media with its national audience, only a handful of senators and even fewer House members are recognized widely enough to serve as "news hooks" around which to focus a story. In the "who, what, where, when, and why" world of journalism, the "who" tends to dominate. If the journalist has to spend too much time explaining who the who is, there is no time left for the rest of the story. They tend to fall back on the established regular cast of characters, giving the wheel another spin—expanding their visibility and increasing the likelihood that they will be sought out as a spokesperson in the future. On the hill, Brian "saw firsthand how difficult it is for any public official to be heard fairly over the electronic media."[40]

Dominick's challenge to Vice President Agnew and, eventually, his Senate seat fell victim to his health problems. In the next election, Dominick lost his seat to Democrat Gary Hart. By that time, Brian was far gone from Dominick's staff.

Although he had no specific plan, Brian felt strongly that there had to be a way to expand the number of voices that could be effectively heard in the American political dialogue. He argued "that when you elect somebody to office, that somebody ought to have the opportunity to talk to his or her constituents without a filter being applied."[41]

As he observed Congress from the inside, he became fascinated, but also began to realize that network television was not showing the real story. His "gut instinct at the time was that if I'm interested enough to want to know more of what's going on behind the scenes, there's got to be some more who feel the same way."[42] Trust in the public's interest in public affairs became a seed that would germinate a decade later.

A STINT AS A POLICY WONK

Brian next became an assistant to Clay T. Whitehead, the director of the Nixon White House Office of Telecommunications Policy (OTP), focusing on legislative relations. Brian's interest was in the technology and its use, not in supporting Nixon per se. For decades, his association with Richard Nixon haunted him among those who questioned his political objectivity. In politics, you are known by the company you keep—or seem to keep. The link with Nixon was pretty tenuous, since, as Brian likes to point out, he never met the man until more than two decades later when he interviewed him on the air.

The Nixon administration arrived with a fervent desire to change telecommunications policy in America. Clay T. Whitehead (Tom to his friends) was put in charge of the Office of Telecommunications Policy, tasked with breaking the stranglehold the networks had on television and saw cable television as the primary vehicle. As Whitehead's assistant for media and congressional relations, Brian not only developed substantive knowledge of the American media environment, but also expanded his list of personal friends and Washington contacts. Antonin Scalia, who later went on to the Supreme Court, served as general counsel to OTP.

Brian's long-term interest in bridging the gap between Washington and the rest of the country got a boost from his growing knowledge of emerging technology. Well beyond the audiotapes shipped back to his parents from Brian's Navy adventures, satellite transmission offered the opportunity to inexpensively transmit television signals. Brian saw it as a way to get beyond the monopoly of the three major networks. Clay Whitehead had the same vision. Brian remembers their goal was to "open up the opportunity to have cheap transmission from Washington to every other city in the United States." Up to that point, only the networks could afford the high cost of using telephone lines. "When the satellite was launched . . . people began to dream about doing other things."[43] Brian fully shared Nixon's distrust of big government and monopoly, at least when it came to the media. Clay Whitehead worked to strip the monopoly of the three networks, primarily through creating a domestic satellite system that would dramatically expand the number of communications channels. When television began, government intentionally favored just three networks with the goal of having some competition, but with a paternalistic desire to make sure they were all commercially viable. Whitehead and his staff realized that with emerging satellite technology, cheap national transmission of television signals was now possible. The largest barrier to a domestic satellite system was the existing networks who feared competition and AT&T, which made millions from current transmission technology.

OTP was under pressure to toe the Nixon White House line. Brian steered clear of the more partisan efforts of Whitehead to slash public affairs funding of the Public Broadcasting System. No president, including Nixon, cared much about telecommunications policy in the abstract; Whitehead saw increasing the options as a way to "stick it in the eye of the existing media," which he felt was too liberal and elitist. Whitehead and his staff used the passion of the Nixon White House to promote their own agenda of increasing options. As Brian put it, "We were a block down the street from the White House, but might as well have been 55 miles away. We constantly played the game of wanting to be close, until things got nasty."

In-house OTP lawyer, Antonin Scalia, was also deeply committed to expanding media choice. The friendship would prosper. Brian found him to be "one of the most ethical people I know." Brian became the godfather to one of Scalia's children. The friendship involved visits to each other's homes even after Scalia continued on his fast track to the Supreme Court. A few decades later, their professional passions would collide over public access to the courts, but their friendship remains. Another young lawyer Brian met at OTP, Henry Goldberg, would provide him with invaluable service in his challenge against the existing media mix.

The time at OTP provided a good graduate degree in media economics under changing technological opportunities. Brian now calls it "my Ph.D." He recalled, "You could begin to see how you could put something together that didn't require megabucks. I'd been taught all my life that this was a democracy, and that many voices were better than a few voices, and I just kept learning that by being part of the system where there were very few voices."[44] He remembers learning at OTP that even the media "was all about money." Brian became more interested in competition and diversity than in particular content. He felt that with more choices, the quality would have room to flourish. Under the existing limited system with the three networks playing a high-priced game, they would gravitate toward the least valuable content. Without choice, Brian concluded, "I will go to my grave underestimating the garbage people will watch."

As the tentacles of Watergate began closing in around the Nixon White House, all of the supporting agencies became entangled. The taint of presidential deceit undermined virtually every policy initiative. Brian had little desire to hold out to the very end. If policy was not moving, it was time for him to move on. As the Nixon administration began to crumble under the weight of Watergate, Brian's frustration grew. OTP, under the inspiration of Clay Whitehead, developed into a 60-person, think tank designed to break open media in America to create more options for the audience. By early 1974, "Watergate made it a mess. Decisions were not being made." Brian felt the wheels spin and planned to get out. Always the loyal worker, he delayed his departure until a major study came out. In his words, "I left OTP because I was sick and tired of government, and I was sick and tired of Richard Nixon."[45]

THE KING IS DEAD, LONG LIVE THE KING

The presidency is more than the president. The office and its functions are too important to depend on the weaknesses and peccadilloes of a particular incumbent. While a presidential administration may look like a well-oiled machine in the service of a president, more often, it is a set of competing fiefdoms serving numerous masters and competing goals. The White House is rife with secrets, and Brian found himself in the middle of a unique and significant one. In the spring of 1974, Richard Nixon's hold on the presidency was beginning to slip. The illegal break-in of the Democratic National Committee headquarters at the Watergate complex was edging closer and closer to his doorstep, while responsibility for the cover-up clearly crossed the threshold. Nixon's unelected vice president, Gerald Ford, lacked a clear political base outside his former congressional district in Michigan. Honest and low-key, Ford was more of an observer than a player in the downfall of Nixon. Philip Buchen, Ford's former law partner and "perennial advisor to Ford throughout his Congressional years,"[46] had returned to Washington from Grand Rapids to serve as chief counsel to the Domestic Council Committee on the Right to Privacy.

As is often the case, proximity is providence. The OTP operated in the same building as the Domestic Council, and Buchen had struck up a friendship with Clay Whitehead. Highly protective of his friend and mentor Gerald Ford, Buchen came to the conclusion that Nixon was on the way out, and Ford could be caught short without some planning. He needed some Washington insiders and had few contacts. At a dinner at Whitehead's home, Buchen proposed a secret planning group. This act of personal loyalty lacked either the blessing or knowledge of Ford. As a Nixon appointee, Whitehead was hesitant, but was persuaded by Buchen's argument that "Jerry needs some kind of planning underway. The president may resign before or after he is impeached. We've got to do some kind of contingency planning."[47] With offices across the hall, Buchan and Whitehead could "confer, without raising eyebrows."[48]

In May 1974, Buchan and Whitehead recruited three acquaintances, all in their mid-thirties: Jonathan Moore, an aide to New York governor Nelson Rockefeller and attorney general Elliot Richardson; Larry Lynn, a former National Security Council staff member; and Brian Lamb, Whitehead's recently departed assistant.[49] Starting a new media career as editor of *The Media Report*, Brian could not shake his attachment to Whitehead. The call recruiting him as part of a secret Ford transition briefing team was nothing he desired or sought. He remembers, "I didn't want to do it. I did it out of loyalty to Tom."

Brian now took on the uncomfortable role of an inside player. The Saturday morning meetings in the kitchen of Whitehead's Georgetown house were dubbed the "Ford Foundation." And they proceeded at a leisurely pace, under the assumption that the Watergate denouement remained many months away. "The five men sat around Whitehead's dining-room table, drinking Cokes."[50] Ford was never aware of the group or its preparations. Hounded by reporters about plans for a transition being carried out by his staff, Ford reacted to a newspaper report of such a group by saying, "If they are, they are doing it without my knowledge and without my consent."[51] Buchan was under no compulsion to correct Ford since none of the participants were technically on the vice president's staff.[52] While some might have interpreted this as a cease-and-desist order, Whitehead and the team interpreted it in just the opposite way. The conspirators concluded that the vice president was saying he "hoped someone was doing it, but he didn't want to know about it."[53]

Brian remembers the four planning sessions as academic seminars on the presidency, where we would discuss "a new president's main difficulty in the first . . . thirty days."[54] The efforts resulted in a sixteen-page working paper titled, "The First Week." While most of the recommendations were organizational, they did take on key personnel issues, such as the suggestion of letting White House Chief of Staff Alexander Haig go.[55] The team expressed concerned about General Haig's capacity to beguile. When Former Secretary of Defense Laird's name surfaced, he was described as charming, intelligent, and an incorrigible schemer.[56] Brian was getting a crash course in high-level personnel evaluation.

Brian's one solo recommendation sounded better on paper than it worked out in practice. Depending on his familiarity with the Washington press corps, Brian was asked who Ford should appoint as press secretary and he recommended Jerald ter Horst, a Michigan journalist trusted by Ford and well-liked by the media with whom he would work. At least part of Nixon's problem stemmed from the rocky relationship between Nixon's press secretary and the media.

Recognizing the sensitivity of the task, Brian accepted the bond of secrecy. None of his friends or family knew of his involvement. He jokes that the initiative was "probably the only kept secret in Washington."[57] After a few days of around-the-clock work, there was little elation. For Brian: "It may sound like an exciting experience, but we were emotionally drained. He (Nixon) let us down. Even if he had committed no crime which could be proven." Careful not to sound boastful, Brian summarizes his experience by saying, "I guess it's patriotic. It was obviously a very meaningful experience. I guess it will be a footnote in history. I was honored I was asked."[58]

SURPRISE AND COUNTERSURPRISE

A few days before Nixon's resignation, Buchen had dinner with the Fords. Things were moving much faster than anyone had expected. Buchen remembers, "We had no notion the thing [resignation] would come up as soon as it did."[59] Ford pulled Buchen aside, conspiratorially saying, "Phil, I want you to keep this confidential, but I think this will be over in 72 hours or less." Thinking the bombshell about Nixon resigning would trump anything else, Ford was astonished when Buchen explained that a transition team had been meeting for the last three months. Their effort resulted in a set of foot-thick notebooks of suggestions. Ford recognized the political danger these people had placed themselves in, but seemed appreciative of the effort and asked Buchen to expand the group to include more Washington heavy hitters.[60]

The expansion included Donald Rumsfeld, a former Republican congressman from Michigan and currently U.S. ambassador to NATO. Brian and Whitehead met with Rumsfeld shortly after he raced back to Washington to help his old colleague. Far from receiving a cordial greeting as backfield players who saved the game, Rumsfeld "was so rude to us. He didn't care what we'd done. Couldn't have cared less." Rumsfeld blew right past the two, without even taking the briefing book.[61] A "safety" copy was given to Phil Buchen to hand-deliver to Ford since Whitehead realized the initial copies would simply gather dust on some shelf.

The secret planning group, of which Brian was a part, is credited with setting the stage for Ford's first few weeks in office. Specifically, they recommended the conciliatory tone of his first address to the nation, his pledge to consider amnesty for draft evaders, reaching out to Black and female members of Congress, and journeys to Capitol Hill and the Department of Health, Education, and Welfare. Ford also accepted their advice to increase openness of the presidency and to lower the level of partisanship.[62] The new president accepted the suggestion to separate the jobs of national security advisor and secretary of state, positions both held by Henry Kissinger in the Nixon Administration.

It must have been a heady experience, for among the recommendations Ford followed, was Brian's recommendation of ter Horst as press secretary. Only a few days after his appointment, ter Horst resigned in protest of Ford's pardon of Richard Nixon. While hindsight suggests Ford's wisdom, the action tore Washington apart. Brian's frustration was directed more at ter Horst than Nixon or Ford, finding the action grandstanding over an issue too unimportant for resignation. Even more troubling for Brian, he had become part of the story more than an observer.[63]

A RICKETY BRIDGE TORN DOWN

Brian's only real venture directly into the political world occurred in the mid-1970s when he considered running against a widely accepted inferior member of Congress, Earl Landgrebe. Landgrebe stuck with Richard Nixon until the very end, eventually proclaiming, "Don't confuse me with the facts."[64] The day before Nixon left office, Langrebe proclaimed, "I'm going to stick with my president even if he and I have to be taken out of this building and shot."[65] Brian's father and uncle had been very political and this seemed like a great opportunity to take on a faltering incumbent. Meeting with the local Republican chair, Clyde Lewis, Brian was flatly told, "We don't take sides in primaries." Support from the party was absolutely necessary in Brian's mind. He concluded, "If the party is going to continue to support this Bozo, I don't want to have anything to do with it." Ever polite, Brian still kept his appointment with the former occupant of the seat and House Minority Leader, Charlie Halleck. The lesson from the Halleck visit had less to do with running for office in central Indiana than with recognizing how quickly the mighty fall. Arriving at 10:00 AM, Brian found Halleck in his "sad house with a gin in his hand." He recognized that it probably was not the first drink of the day. For Brian, "it was a reality test and something I did not want to repeat."

GOING LEGIT IN PRINT

In 1974, Barbara Ruger hired Brian to do a column for *CATV Weekly*. The job was less important than the exposure. Ruger sold Brian on the idea by saying, "You come with us, and we'll put your picture on the column." It was not so much that he was looking to boost his ego, but rather to become known in the cable industry. As Brian put it, "I'd write my column with my picture on it . . . a couple of years later, everybody knew who I was in the business. And then I started to go to them and say, "What do you think about my idea for C-SPAN?"[66] Repeating his high school strategy of using his journalism credentials as an entrée, Brian used his column at *CATV Weekly* to interview the big guys on the block. When he heard that CBS newsman Mike Wallace had been invited to speak at the Cable Television Convention in 1976, Brian picked up the phone in his home office and asked for in interview. Much to his surprise, Wallace said yes, as long as he could get up to New York in an hour and a half. Brian grabbed his tape recorder, dashed to National Airport, took the shuttle and got the interview.

Wallace turned out not to have many ideas about cable television and, when challenged, thought *60 Minutes* had covered the issue pretty well. As Wallace was showing Brian around the office, Morley Safer returned from a late lunch. Wallace introduced Brian; Wallace told Safer that "he said we don't cover cable television because we're in the broadcasting business." Brian remembers that "Morley was a little loose at that point, and he looked up to me and said, 'You know, he's god-damned right.'"[67]

Brian's predilections show like a flashlight on a dark night. He not only wants to guide his own way, but also provide guidance to others. As Stan Searle, his boss at *CATV Weekly* put it, "You know the problem with Brian Lamb—He wants to make a difference." He treated each of his media jobs as graduate courses on the media environment and diagnostic opportunities for discovering ways to change media delivery.

In 1976, Brian moved from *CATV Weekly* to Washington Bureau Chief for *Cablevision,* the trade magazine for the cable industry. It looked like a sweetheart deal. The $42,000 salary was princely compared to his past jobs, and Bob Titsch, owner of *Cablevision,* committed support for Brian's emerging goal of creating a public affairs network. The new position provided access to the thinking and operations of the nation's top cable executives. As the cable operator's gatekeeper to their colleagues, few turned down his requests for interviews. While the access remained, Brian's taste of a guaranteed good salary fell by the wayside. Titsch gave Brian enough rope to succeed or hang himself. Within a year, his workload and his salary were cut in half to allow him time to develop *Cable Video,* a public affairs service that involved producing videotaped interviews with members of Congress. The concept looked simple. Brian and his one-man camera crew—his fellow reporter at *Cablevision,* Pat Grisham—carried out short interviews with members on the steps of the Capitol. The tapes would then be sent to cable systems in their district for airing. The concept satisfied the motivations of all participants. Members of Congress regularly sought to "advertise" themselves and their initiatives.[68] Cable operators needed unique programming to justify the expense of subscribing. Brian saw the fifteen-minute interviews as a significant improvement over the sound-bite coverage that usually flew under the banner of public affairs programming.

In addition, he continued to publish *The Media Report,* designed to cover the media like the media covers everyone else. Some reporters are conduits, taking in information, processing, and expelling it. They know little more when they are finished than when they began; they fear clogging up their minds will make it more difficult to process the next story. Brian, on the other hand, lives to learn. He described his time at *Cablevision* as "allowing me to get to know the major figures in the business and to study the industry. It was like going to school."[69]

The first *Cable Video* interview subject would prove fortuitous later. Not satisfied with chance, Brian sought out Lionel Van Deerlin (D-CA), chairman of the powerful House Subcommittee on Communications. As a former newspaper and television journalist, Van Deerlin understood Brian's goals and harbored a soft spot for the emerging cable industry. The positive response to programs resulted in securing grants from fifteen cable operators for additional interviews. Tape distribution followed a retail model, passed around from cable operator to cable operator in a system called "bicycling." Brian proved the interest in public affairs programming, but needed a more efficient wholesale method of distribution.

BRIAN'S PERSONAL BRIDGE SPANNING LESSONS

Brian Lamb's initial decade in Washington left him with a perceptual screen that would guide his behavior for the bulk of the rest of his career. These chunks of understanding would guide his success and feed his frustrations. They include:

- The criteria for defining newsworthiness panders to the audiences with sound bites, celebrity, and irrelevant controversy.
- Societal policy debate is dominated by too few and too homogeneous voices.
- Follow the money: The media is driven by a financial bottom line, not one based on professional ethics or the good of society.
- The "flyover" states of the Midwest are shortchanged in the policy dialogue.
- A strong feeling that government control limits the quality and range of news.
- Public officials have tremendous advantages in manipulating the news.
- News persons and politicians underestimate the knowledge and interest of the public.

4

BUILDING BRIDGE SUPPORTS

Politicians are the same all over. They promise to build a bridge even where there is no river.

—Nikita Khrushchev

WHO NEEDS A NEW BRIDGE ANYWAY?

Brian Lamb is an unlikely revolutionary, but like revolutionaries of the past, he is willing to take on established institutions. His approach is indirect rather than frontal. He simply provides an alternative that he hopes will challenge some of the commercial television networks' power. Brian explained that from 1963 to about 1983, the commercial television news organizations had an overwhelming amount of power. "That was probably not the way the forefathers would have liked it. We were force-feeding the masses with three newscasts because they wanted to watch TV, not because they wanted to watch news."[1]

Seeing the media from a number of different perspectives changed Brian, leading him to conclude, "My experiences with Washington coverage at the Pentagon and on Capitol Hill led me to believe that there had to be a better way to cover public affairs." He recognized that network television was not showing the nation what was really happening in national politics. His "gut instinct at the time was that if I'm interested enough to want to know more of what's going on behind the scenes, there's got to be some more who feel the same way."[2] Brian is uncomfortable being called a visionary. He is much more modest, explaining that his interest "came more out of frustration than any great vision."[3]

The germ of Brian's idea emerged from his personal experience. He readily admits that "it was probably the result of growing up in Lafayette and studying journalism and then going to the big city and thinking, 'Gee, there's a lot missing here. . . . That's not the way I was taught'; I felt a sense that there was another way to do it."[4]

Brian's frustration with the developing media landscape in America festered. Unlike many observers, he tends not to point fingers at either the audience or the media itself. He blames most of the shortcomings on the government that decided to allocate very few channels in order to reduce competition with the intention of guaranteeing profitability to each. The three networks gravitated "to the lowest common denominator," relegating the ten percent of public affairs to commercially undesirable time periods.[5] Brian became a great believer in deregulation and the ability of the market to sort out the best and worst programs.

Those who teach social studies and civics, whether formally in the classroom or informally in the public forum, face a double-edged sword. Too much glorification of the contemporary political system may raise expectations and lead to frustration. Too much condemnation of the current system's shortcomings may turn listeners into disenchanted and apathetic citizens. As a civic practitioner, Brian attempted to confront reality and then *do* something about it. He explains, "I'd been taught all my life that this was a democracy and that many voices were better than a few voices . . . and I just kept learning by being part of the system that there were very few voices."[6]

Carrying over his experience in the Office of Telecommunications Policy, Brian started from the assumption that "Both Democrats and Republicans in Congress distrusted big media, big power, and the networks. And they both wanted especially to reduce the power of big media to manipulate public policy."[7]

THE MARRIAGE BROKER

Building a bridge between Washington and the public required acquiring assent from a number of different players. Like a good marriage broker, Brian recognized that self-interest trumps altruism. The attributes of each potential partner must emerge as contributory to the self-interest of the other potential partners. The plain daughter is described as "solid and hardworking," while the lazy son is credited with being "laid back and pleasant." Potential partnerships are described as "matches made in heaven," or "the joining of two wonderful families." While the rhetoric of the courtship dance may emphasize grand goals and principles, the potential partners hope to see their self-interests reflected, at least obliquely, in advantages of the proposed future state the marriage broker outlines. Potential partners are generally more interested in the physical attraction, financial potential, and/or promise of healthy and good-looking children that might emerge from the match than in abstract goals.

Brian's life has constantly been one of looking forward while looking back. As he explored forging relationships with the House leadership and national cable moguls, he also reached back to his former boss Dick Shively, who, along with a number of local cable operators, had created the Cable Satellite Access Entry group. They realized that in order to get increased cable subscriptions, they needed a "value added" argument. In areas of the country where physical barriers mitigated against receiving any signal without cable, no problem existed. On the other hand, for much of the country where regular reception sufficed, cable subscriptions had to be sold on the basis of exclusive access to new programming. Brian arrived at the group's meeting at the Mayflower Hotel in Washington, D.C., with the only truly new idea, a public affairs network. All of the other presenters simply wanted to recycle old movies.

Brian's task in putting together the partnership necessary to launch C-SPAN followed the tried and true pattern of coalition building. The public debate emphasized transcendent values associated with democracy and citizen education, while potential partners whispered among each other a narrower set of goals. Members of Congress cared more about controlling and improving their image than in making some abstract contribution to democracy. Members of the cable industry were looking for expanded programming that would enhance the value of their product and were not unaware of the fact that it might be a good thing to keep on the good side of Congress, which regulated their industry. Brian cannot be left on the playing field as the only true altruist. He obviously saw success as a ticket to future employment in a quest he enjoyed. Even the pursuit of an altruistic goal has some self-interest involved for the pursuer. He or she gains a sense of self-satisfaction for doing the right thing.

It is not fair to completely denigrate self-interested behavior. Some great advances have emerged from self-interest. Impressive initiatives, such as the U.S. Constitution, the Bill of Rights, the Voting Rights Act, and the United Nations Charter, were all pervaded by individuals whose self-interests were molded and channeled into a product that was better and more farsighted than their individual initial self-interests might have provided for. Effective coalitions require compromise of one's self interest in order to make the outcome palatable to all the partners. Congress had to give some control, either allowing the cameras on all the time or none of it. Congress would not become a producer, offering a package of self-serving clips. The cable companies had to commit funds and channel capacity.

BUILDING SUPPORT STRUT BY STRUT

One of Brian's early C-SPAN colleagues points out, "It was like *Mr. Smith Goes to Washington*," the 1939 Frank Capra movie featuring Jimmy Stewart taking on Washington single-handedly with little support except that of the public. "Brian is really a populist and a democrat with a small 'd.' He really believes in the system. . . . Brian is one of the least cynical people you'll ever meet. . . . He was careful not to let them [his cable colleagues] know how strongly he felt about it—how idealistic it was. . . . My advice to him was . . . 'Turn it down a little, because you are going to scare these guys off.'" An early backer from the cable industry agrees, saying that "Brian had a burning intensity and a vision that was more in his gut than in his head. . . . There are few times when one person makes a difference, and Brian Lamb did that."

Cable operators remember Brian selling C-SPAN to reluctant owners "like the oil-filter salesman who says if you don't get it for your car now, you'll have to get it later. . . . He was always on their backs."[8]

ROADBLOCKS

Entrepreneurs are almost by definition risk takers. If something is easy to do and offers many benefits, someone else would have done it. Entrepreneurs see the world as it might be as opposed to what it is. Some risk money, some security, and some risk fame. The fear of failure dissuades many. Brian's down-to-earth view of himself insulated him from some of the downsides of risk. He looks back and says, "The risks weren't significant. No one knew who I was. If I failed, so what."[9]

Lacking audience surveys, focus groups, or any other sort of data, Brian promoted C-SPAN on hope and an assumption. He explains, "I just had a gut feeling that enough people were as interested as I was in government, so we could find our niche." Brian's presumption was not met with open arms. Most people he pitched the idea to failed to agree. As he remembers, "The overall reaction to the [idea] of the channel was that it was really a silly idea. They would say, 'why would people want to watch that stuff?'"10

As cable operator Robert Titsch, Sr. explains it, "Brian was driven by the dream. . . . He felt that the American public was getting screwed by television. He felt that the government—the most powerful government in the world—was hidden from its constituents and that the people should see it."11 One variant of a dream is a nightmare. Brian admits that he was "really angry about the power of the networks," who failed to provide a fair or adequate picture of the political process.

There was no magic moment when Brian's rationale or passion overcame opposition. Brian remembers "a tremendous amount of rejection. . . . People would pat me on the head and say, 'Nice little boy, keep it up Brian.'"12 Brian's audience was tough and varied. Cable television started out as a gaggle of mom-and-pop operators running on a shoestring, as opposed to the current large corporations. They were not accustomed to large and risky expenditures with no guarantee of immediate payback. As Continental Cablevision's Amos B. Hostetter Jr. describes it, "These people were not Time Warner or Cox Broadcasting. They were small-town appliance dealers who put an antenna up on a hill and brought a wire down from there to hook up your television set up, so they could sell you the television set."13

PUTTING THOUGHT INTO ACTION

While the idea of a public affairs network had been bouncing around his head for years, Brian first formally presented the idea of a television network devoted to politics in 1977 to forty cable operators at the Mayflower Hotel. Using his entrée as Washington Chief for *CableVision* magazine, Brian had already run the concept by Bob Rosencrans, who ran the Madison Square Garden Sports network, which had plenty of satellite time when sports events were not going on. The cable industry was looking for new ideas for programming that would make cable more appealing and the organizer of the group gave Brian twenty minutes to pitch his idea to "see if anybody was interested."14 As a reporter for *Cablevision* magazine, he was well-known by his audience, yet he had little idea whether they would buy his vision. As one colleague put it, no one wanted to tee him off, because "they didn't want to get carved up in the pages." Many operators silently thought, "You know, this nice guy, he's got this nutty idea, it doesn't make any economic sense at all, but he's *CableVision* magazine, so what the hell."

On the surface, the potential looked slim. Here Brian was, facing a bunch of hardened businessmen who thought in terms of the bottom line. Their shoestring operations were not big enough to allow a lot of risky experimentation. By his own admission, he recognized that "I was over my head from the beginning. I didn't know business, had never run anything."[15]

PUTTING YOUR MONEY WHERE YOUR MOUTH IS

After a thirty-minute presentation, Brian recalls, "Most of the operators looked at me like I'd been smoking something."[16] The exceptions were Bob Rosencrans and Ken Gunter, who responded with, "We think this is neat. Maybe we can help you."[17] Brian looks back at Rosencrans as his "sugar daddy," who was not only the first to ante up, but went out to sell the idea to his cable colleagues. In Brian's words, "Bob's support of C-SPAN was total. He never blinked, never gave an excuse."[18] Rosencrans went on to become the first chair of C-SPAN's board of directors.

The money came with strings attached; Rosencrans told Brian, "You need to write a business plan." Brian admits that he had "no idea what a business plan was." At the suggestion of developing a business plan, Brian responded, with a blank look remembering that, "I had no clue what he was talking about. I would just as soon go in the bathroom and throw up as to try and write a business plan."[19] Not willing to let Brian and his investment fail, Rosencrans invited Brian to his house in Connecticut the week before Christmas. Rosencrans contributed more than money, serving as his de facto professor in "business principles 101." In a crash course on what businessmen expect, Brian learned about market analysis, marketing, financial projections, and operating plans. It was not rocket science, but it had never been part of Brian's bag of tricks.

Brian's National Cable Satellite Corporation (NCSC) existed more on paper and in Brian's head more than anything else. The $25,000 Rosencrans contributed as an affiliate fee would not go very far, and Brian needed to reach out to other cable operators. His money served as seed money designed to convince other operators of the value of the project.[20] Brian touts this experience to show how one person can change the future, remarking that Rosencrans was "that one human who made all the difference."[21] Within two weeks, Brian had collected $400,000 from twenty-two operators. Others donated labor, materials, satellite time, and equipment necessary to move the project forward.[22]

TAKING A LUNCH BREAK *AND* A CONCRETE ANCHOR

The financial vote of confidence in creating a public affairs network said little about the content. No one clearly remembers that magic moment when the light went on and the future path shown brightly. In retrospect, John Kennedy's (probably borrowed) quote that "success has a thousand fathers, and failure is an orphan," helps explain the memories of many of Brian's friends that they were there at *the* founding. In Brian's mind, many people played key roles in completing the initial puzzle. One of the key meetings occurred at the West Park hotel overlooking Washington, D.C., with John Evans, an old Navy colleague and president of the Arlington, Virginia, cable company. After reminiscing about their time at the Pentagon and their frustration with the government's ability to use the media and reduce public access, the conversation turned to solutions. The magnificent view of Washington obviously spawned expansive thoughts. Evans remembers that "We were talking about democracy and to what extent people need to participate in order for it to work."[23] News that the House was considering installing television cameras led Evans to consider putting its proceedings up on his local system. "Wouldn't it be interesting if I could get that signal and put it on my cable system?"[24] The opportunity hit Brian like a lightning bolt.

It was not a far step to think in terms of putting coverage of the House up on a satellite for the entire cable industry. With over 1,800 hours in session spread over more than 300 days, the reservoir of guaranteed programming was impressive. The House could serve as the programming anchor for a public affairs network.

Evan's pressing problem lay delivering the thirty-six channels to the first cable system in the Washington, D.C. area. He recognized that the proximity to Washington would increase the scrutiny from an important segment of the Washington establishment. Numerous members of Congress lived in his coverage area. They would undoubtedly find coverage of their endeavors appealing.

OH, FATEFUL DAY

On October 27, 1977, Brian, as part of his *Cablevision* job, conducted an interview with Lionel Van Deerlin (D-CA), chairman of the House Interstate and Foreign Commerce Committee, Subcommittee on Communications.

The House had already been discussing providing a live feed of floor proceedings, but lacked an acceptable distribution plan. They worried about simply giving it to the networks, who they knew would cut it into sound bites and broadcast only the most conflict laden and/or embarrassing moments. During the interview, Brian mentioned that cable television could broadcast the proceedings in their entirety. Van Deerlin, a journalist before entering the House, jumped on the idea eagerly and asked Brian, "Could you write a speech for me?" Brian remembers the moment with mixed emotions. In one sense, "That was the magic moment where it all kind of coalesced." On the other hand, as a journalist employed by the cable industry, he thought, "Boy, there's a conflict of interest."

Recognizing that debate on the issue would not take place for two weeks, Brian savored his ability to interject his idea into the political process, using his promise to "think about" writing the speech as a way of buying time on the ethical issue. While the political gristmill can grind quite slowly, that proved not to be the case on this issue. By the time Brian got back to his office, Van Deerlin was on the phone telling him that he loved the idea and asked Brian to immediately write a speech for him to deliver, "You are not going to believe this, but this thing's on the floor right now. If you want this stuff on the record, give it to me over the phone, and I'll write it down and go out on the floor and make a speech."[25] It was a case of "speak now, or forever hold your peace." Brian swallowed any ethical concerns and fed Van Deerlin some ideas and numbers in the twenty-minute conversation that followed. Van Deerlin "literally walked to the floor of the House, right then, and gave a speech off the top of his head."[26]

Van Deerlin's speech emphasized the value of cable as the distribution method, arguing that gavel-to-gavel coverage on cable "will be available at times and to an extent that no commercial station, certainly not network, could or would provide. But they might easily be included within the new channel capability of a cable operator."[27]

The House voted 325 to 40 to allow television coverage and delegated to Speaker of the House Thomas "Tip" O'Neill (D-MA) the power to determine the specific methods of implementation.

Van Deerlin's speech about cable distribution caught the Speaker and his staff off guard. Van Deerlin received a call from one of his aides saying, "The Speaker wants to know what the hell you were talking about yesterday."[28] Van Deerling threw the hot potato in Brian's direction and stepped back.

MASTER OF THE HOUSE

The project would go nowhere without the support of Speaker Tip O'Neill, an old-time Democratic politician, who believed in controlling "his" chamber. Large in size, ego, and power, O'Neill remained a throwback to old style backroom politics, not surprising for someone cutting his political teeth in the union halls and ethnic neighborhoods of Boston. More comfortable in private huddles than on public display, O'Neill harbored little trust in the news media. As he explained it, "We were disgusted with how the major networks covered the Republican and Democratic national conventions. If a guy was reading a newspaper, they'd always show a close-up of him. If a delegate was picking his nose or scratching his ass, that's what you would see. If somebody had a bald head, you could be sure of getting a close-up view of the shiny spot. No wonder so many of us were skittish. After all, why should the greatest legislative body in the world allow itself to be demeaned and humiliated before millions of people."[29]

Brian recognized that coalitions are built by tapping the unique motivations of each necessary partner. Brian's brief January 1978 meeting with Speaker O'Neill proved anticlimactic. It was a done deal, worked out by his staff charged with carrying out the details. Unlike most government deals, the agreement to provide gavel-to-gavel coverage relied on a verbal commitment, but no written contract. O'Neill showed relatively little interest. As Brian describes the scene, "I didn't talk anyone into anything. The only thing I did was to solidify the agreement and take a picture to show industry commitment." The deal gave O'Neill plenty of room to recognize that gavel-to-gavel coverage would give him a chance to "spit in the eye of the networks"[30] whose sound-bite coverage of the House so frustrated him. In his gut, O'Neill retained some hesitance, fearing how the new medium would treat him and the institution he loved. A few years later, he would rue the day the cameras arrived. Gary Hymel, a key O'Neill aide, points out that C-SPAN's financial autonomy made it more acceptable as well, since it was important to maintain clear a separation from Congress.[31] With O'Neill's blessing, Brian was sent out on the street to sell it to the cable operators. In a world of contracts and lawyers, Brian's agreement to provide gavel-to-gavel coverage was completely verbal. It is a commitment that has not been breeched in the network's almost thirty years of coverage.

OVER TO YOU

Brian's commitment to O'Neill lacked the blessing of the cable operators. He was out on a slim guy-wire over a broad chasm. It was not a
"slam dunk" easy sell. Some operators turned him down flat. The cable
operators were independent businesspersons who had not achieved success by throwing their money away. Others were intrigued, as in the
words of Bob Rosencrans of Columbia U.S. Cablevision, who saw the
network as "the basis of developing a whole new reason for people to be
interested in cable."[32] Others reflected a more pragmatic, "you scratch my
back and I'll scratch yours" motivation, hoping that by broadcasting the
House, they would build political credits in an institution charged with
regulating their endeavors.

Brian ended up back on the street pleading for money. Going hat-in-
hand to ask for money, especially from hardened businesspersons tests the
mettle of even the most idealistic petitioners. Russell Karp, founder to
Teleprompter, was big, both physically and in the cable business. Almost a
foot taller than Brian, at 6'5", Karp flatly turned down the idea of *Cable
Video* for his Manhattan clientele. Undaunted, Brian sought him out for his
new venture. Staking out the hearing room where Karp would testify, Brian
screwed up his courage and caught him as he emerged. Brian blurted out,
"Mr. Karp, you may not remember me, but I'm the guy who approached
you with the *Cable Video* idea that you didn't think was so great. Well, I have
another idea now. I want to provide live gavel-to-gavel coverage of the
House of Representatives in session." While the hesitation was probably
only momentary, it must have seemed like an eon to Brian. The next thing
he knew, Karp had stopped in his tracks and said, "What a great idea. You
know if we had that in 1964, we would never have gotten into the Vietnam War. You've got my support."

PUTTING THE SATELLITES WHERE HIS MOUTH WAS

As the House moved toward installing cameras, Brian was faced with getting commitments from the cable operators he had promised the Speaker
without their knowledge. Brian, the good Boy Scout, learned the importance of always being prepared. He threw out ideas and made commitments
about cable industry support, even though he had not received any formal
authority from the cable operators. Now Brian had to scramble to make the
cable distribution happen.

PAYING THE TOLL

Creating C-SPAN was an all-consuming activity, leaving Brian with little time for anything else. As is usually the case, his half-time job with *Cable Vision* took up more than half his time. If one ever wants more than one full-time employee, hire two half-time ones. Throughout his career Brian's personal life tended to get short shrift. As one of Brian's friends put it, "Brian always had a woman in his life, but never seemed to have the time to have *the* woman in his life." During the mid-1970s, he did show how he could reorder his priorities when necessary. When his girlfriend at the time went through cancer and a mastectomy, Brian was right at her side at the hospital. When the young woman recovered, the relationship fell by the wayside.

FROM LONE RANGER TO TEAM CAPTAIN

As C-SPAN developed, it was overseen by a 22-member board of directors. The cable operators were not going to trust "their" airwaves and funds to an eager beaver with an untried idea. Brian's first surprise was that only about ten of them showed a strong commitment to the concept behind his "baby." He eventually resigned himself to the fact that "It's like anything. There were 55 delegates selected to the first constitutional convention, and only 39 showed up." Even a handpicked board would not include a roomful of zealots. Years later, Lamb would look back saying, "Twenty-five years ago, I was a guy with an idea to give the public access to public events without interruption and without commentary. But C-SPAN is also a story of a group of public-minded cable entrepreneurs who stepped up and said, 'Yes, we'll put the House of Representatives on our cable systems,' and who continue to support us to this day."[33]

Brian's current image as the cool, collected, and laid-back host belies his feelings at early C-SPAN board meetings. As he describes it, "A bunch of fairly sophisticated businessmen were watching an unsophisticated social entrepreneur dance. I wasn't so sure they didn't <u>just</u> want to watch me dance. They made me sweat and worry. They wanted to make darn sure the commitment was there. If they ever thought I wasn't totally committed, they would be out in a flash. For the first couple of years I didn't sleep past 3:00 AM. I listened to the Larry King show from its inception in 1978 as a diversion, when it started on 28 stations every night. I knew his whole shtick. The drive [to succeed] was everything. I didn't know what I was doing half the time. People thought I was crazy."[34]

LOOKING BACK OVER THE BRIDGE SPAN

By 1979, Brian had built the conceptual bridge, received initial support, and was on his way to spanning the chasm between Washington and "real" America. His success in turning the idea into reality is a testimony to the fact that idealism is not always unrealistic. Brian was clever enough to hitch his wagon to the star of the cable industry, whose motives were based more on regulatory tolerance and economic success, and to members of Congress, who needed publicity and accepted with faith that "to know us is to love us."

5

BUILDING AND STRENGTHENING
THE RICKETY BRIDGE

So he with difficulty and labour hard
Moved on, with difficulty and labour he;
But he once passed, soon after when man fell,
Strange alteration! Sin and Death amain
Following his track, such was the will of Heaven,
Paved after him a broad and beaten way
Over the dark abyss, whose boiling gulf
Tamely endured a bridge of wondrous length
From hell continued reaching th' utmost orb
Of this frail world.

—John Milton, *Paradise Lost* (l. Bk. II, l. 1021–1030)

Civil engineers analyze the strength of materials, test weight limits, and have a pretty good idea of a bridge's capacity. Engineers with foresight anticipate future needs and build today's bridges in such a way that future lanes can be added. They stake their careers on the fact that nothing unexpected will happen. C-SPAN grew without a master plan, but rather had a master planner who took advantage of situations, pushing his staff and equipment to its limit.

BUILDING THE FIRST SPAN

Building in the Washington area in winter offers a challenge under the best of conditions. Today's 60-degree taste of spring more than likely gives way to tomorrow's subfreezing ice storm and the next day's balmy rain. The winter of 1979 strutted its stuff. Most challenging for Washington with its roads crowded for rain and its lack of equipment is snow. The 25 inches of snow that arrived just as building the C-SPAN earth station commenced seemed like a particularly cruel trick. The initial contractor refused to get off the dime, so Brian hired a motley crew from Augusta, Georgia, who took off on the construction task hell-bent for erection. It seemed like one step forward and one step back.

It was one thing to create a concept and another to set it in concrete—literally. In order to broadcast, C-SPAN needed an earth station. It was January 1979, with the first broadcast House session scheduled for March. Securing a piece of land in Fairfax County, Virginia, adjacent to the PBS microwave tower, propelled Brian into a new adventure and potential conflict. While PBS had passed on covering the House under its rules, they had little desire to help out an upstart who might compete with them for audiences. Lacking a staff, Brian served as general contractor, but felt more like an inexperienced private. Challenges, such as water table measurements surveys and setback requirements, filled his days. He spent his time negotiating with PBS, which refused to share their microwave tower and opposed C-SPAN building a new one. He received an education in local politics, presenting his case before the Fairfax City Board of Zoning Appeals and the Fairfax County Board of Zoning Appeals. When the county board chair asked if there were any objections to the 120-foot setback, the PBS representative shot back, "I object." Brian remembers, "I've never been so angry in my life. The hair on the back of my head just stood straight up."[1] PBS lawyers first attempted to block action by the Board. Failing there, PBS placed dramatic limitation on the use of "their" road, even though it had been built with public funds. Brian saw it as "a cheap shot. It was never explained to me what their motives were, but they did everything in their power to stop us from getting underway." PBS had never shown any real interest in broadcasting Congress, "but they did not want to see us do it."

The only way to get to the construction site involved using a road that PBS owned. PBS played hardball, requiring Brian to sign a document limiting the weight of trucks and guaranteeing no harm to the road. The glory of being a power figure in Washington gains a dose of reality when Brian muses, "On the day the trucks brought the concrete, I was dressed in my $9.00 Polish boots supervising trucks, picking up any debris that accidentally fell on the road. PBS did absolutely everything humanly possible to prevent us from building this uplink. PBS today wishes they had done what we did."[2]

Akin to a Perry Mason mystery or an "NCIS" who-dun-it, where a key witness walks into the courtroom at the last moment with the case changing evidence, Brian beat back a challenge from PBS over the setback for the tower, with a piece of information unknown to the opposition. Due to a mistake at the time of the acquisition of the land, C-SPAN owned five extra feet, giving C-SPAN enough land to meet the requirement. The board overruled the objection and granted the permit. Construction was completed only a matter of hours before C-SPAN promised to be on the air.

The first day on the air was a victory for Brian, but not an unvarnished success. Booking a room in the House office buildings, Brian invited members of the cable industry and members of Congress in to watch the initial transmission on televisions set up for that purpose. Given his key role in overseeing House procedures, Representative Jack Brooks, chairman of the U.S. House Committee on Government Operations, was invited by Brian. Inviting Brooks to the microphone, Brian expected congratulations. Instead, acerbic Brooks blurted out, "The House is on television today, no thanks to you god-damned folks." Perhaps, Brian should have realized it as the first salvo in a continuing rocky relationship with the House.

After the first week on the air, C-SPAN supporters from the cable industry hosted a small cocktail party to celebrate the success. When one of his cable supporters commented, "You know when I gave you $25,000, I never thought you'd do it," Brian recognized the shallowness of some of this support. He was tempted to say, "Then why did you give me the money?" but held his tongue.[3]

NOW, HOW DO WE USE THIS BRIDGE?

Brian's dream began with the commitment to broadcast the House, but in his mind, it was not only the House story at stake. Feeds from the House are available to any television network, but after the first day, it was clear that the House made the right decision in casting its lot with C-SPAN. The first day, the major networks used a few clips on the evening news, then largely ignored the availability of the signal unless some verbal fireworks erupted on the floor. PBS bumped Sesame Street to carry the first few hours, but made no plan to return, leaving C-SPAN as the only one there for the duration.

In the early years of operation, C-SPAN eschewed sophisticated production. Brian recalled, "When we started, we had four people [and] no cameras. [We] just flipped the switch over there, added some crawls, to the screen and people's names."[4] Conservative activist Paul Weyrich, one of

Brian's old colleagues on Capitol Hill, was one of the first guests on the new network. He remembers, "During my interview, the blue curtain behind me came crashing down. It was truly live television. Amazingly, however, from day one, there were wall-to-wall phone calls."[5]

In their second set of offices, Brian had a new option—the ability to broadcast programming. The new digs were far from luxurious; secondhand orange dividers from a nearby bank created semi-private offices. The "studio" was created by cleaning off one of the desks in front of a blue backdrop. The initial C-SPAN set was pretty minimal, slapped together with pieces of plywood and carpet from a local hardware store. Although a subject of laughter today, the falling C-SPAN logo was a constant fear of Brian and other early hosts. Brian remembers, "During interviews, I was always looking up behind the guests because sometimes the 'C' would fall off."[6]

PICKING UP STAKES AND MAKING A BIG MOVE

The move from Arlington, Virginia, to Capitol Hill was unsettling for Brian. After years of "fly-by-night" operations, he was not convinced that they would need a 5,000-square-foot (a little more than a basketball court) set of offices and studios. Expanding the available space five times seemed like a rather dramatic step. He told the staff to "keep the doors of the offices we are not using closed, or else we will start using them." A bit embarrassed by the luxury and the size, Brian maintained some of his Midwestern conservatism by saying, "I don't want any of these rooms used right away. The minute we start opening up these rooms, they'll get filled."

The current 40,000 square feet (a little less than a football field) on two floors was inconceivable back in 1981. When Jana Fay began looking into a new phone system, Brian told her to only consider the system that would handle up to forty phones, because "we are never going to be any bigger than that." They went with the forty-phone system, but it turned out not to be enough. The current offices now have over three hundred phone lines. It was more than Brian's Midwestern fiscal conservatism at work. He truly did not want a big organization. He was afraid that with layers of staff, it would "mess up the decision-making process." Having to constantly fight for funds, Brian knew how precarious the whole operation was. He did not want to build a big organization and then have to begin to lay people off.

When designing C-SPAN's new offices, Brian made sure that they all included large glass panels. His includes two. Not only does this arrangement telegraph openness to passersby, it also gives the occupant an idea of what is going on outside his or her own space. Brian did not design a bridge to have him and his staff lock themselves away behind closed door. During one of the interviews for this book, Brian glanced into the hall, jumped up, excused himself, and dashed out to meet the parents of a new employee. The employee was thrilled that she rated such attention, and the parents beamed when the "big boss" took time to recognize their progeny.

Old-timers on the staff are a bit embarrassed by the relative luxury of C-SPAN's current offices on Capitol Hill. The sixth-floor executive suite and production departments with offices and an executive conference room with a panoramic view of the Capitol are impressive even by Washington standards. The people down in the first-floor studios refer to the executive offices as "mahogany row," more out of pride than invidious comparison. Typical to Brian's operating style, his office does not have the premier view. Insiders are quick to point out, "Don't be fooled by our current offices. It wasn't always this way. We used to work out of cubby holes with phones on the floor."

AVOIDING "A BRIDGE OVER TROUBLED WATER"

Brian is a man of his word and expects the same of others. He promised Speaker O'Neill gavel-to-gavel coverage of the House. As C-SPAN went beyond floor coverage to include public affairs events both on Capitol Hill and off, Representative (not to be confused with the television personality) Charles Rose (D-NC), then chairman of the committee overseeing House television, took interest in the expanded coverage. Brian worked hard to make sure programming decisions were fair and balanced. One of Rose's staff members (later his wife and then ex-wife), Joan Teague, sought to assert editorial control over C-SPAN programming, a significant threat backed by the implication that access to House coverage could be denied. Rose sought access to viewer letters and the right to exert editorial control C-SPAN coverage. Brian rebuffed the attempts and made a long-term enemy.

Rose, a self-described "technology gadget freak," took extraordinary interest in new technology. His appointment as the chair of the Speaker's Advisory Committee on Television provided the platform he expected to dominate the process. A key sticking point revolved around C-SPAN's insistence on controlling which committee hearings to cover. C-SPAN uses a relatively objective committee system to choose those hearings for most importance, but that are not covered by the rare appearance of the networks. Rose couched his argument in broad strategic terms asserting, "The power to pick what committee hearings members of Congress watch is the power to set your own legislative agenda."[7] More narrowly, C-SPAN's failure to cover one of Rose's committee hearings created the most irritating thorn in the Congressman's side. Joan Teague complained, "We gave free reign to them and they would not be cooperative. . . . They wouldn't even be here if it wasn't for us."[8] When Rose attempted to require C-SPAN to provide programming to anyone free of charge, Brian countered by asserting that the cable industry had a right to protect its investment. For several months, Rose blocked C-SPAN broadcasts of House proceedings.

Brian was unwilling to play the typical game of paying homage to power and trading political favors.[9] In a town like Washington, where people are known by their enemies, Brian had long stood out as an exception whose enemy list is hard to find. Politics receives its activating force by the whole range of human emotions, from grand philosophical goals to petty personal bickering. The feud between Brian Lamb and Charlie Rose was largely one-sided, but no less virulent. For the first year, Rose would not allow C-SPAN to be broadcast on the House's internal television system. Rose ranted, "C-SPAN is a Republican network. I don't think we should let a right-wing Republican like Brian Lamb decided what is on the House system."[10]

DRIVING THE FOUNDER CRAZY

Brian grew up with a Midwestern ethos that avoided the trendy, adopted change slowly, and eschewed unnecessary expenditures. As one of his old friends explained, "Brian is really frugal," and then, on reconsideration, amended his comments to say, "No, he is really tight." His personal outlook melted into his professional decisions. Brian's old yellow Toyota Corolla hatchback, which doubled as the C-SPAN equipment van and "limousine," stands out as a symbol of the early days. Brian used to save a few bucks in taxi fare by meeting board members at the airport in his hatchback. Some of C-SPAN's board had a hard time understanding Brian's motivation. Most businesspersons take the financial bottom line as the ultimate test of all value. Brian ultimately views his board as a vehicle for guaranteeing carriage of the C-SPAN signal. Expanding cable subscriptions have guaranteed adequate operating funds without forcing the bard to constantly fight for increases. Brian gets embarrassed when board members try to increase his compensation or benefits. Salary increases were accepted only reluctantly.

So, board members try to find other ways to show their appreciation. Cars serve as the personal projection of many people, especially men, implying that if the car is cool, powerful, or manly, so are they. A new board member proposed providing Brian with a car and driver. He was appalled, saying, "I could care less. In fact, there are too many individuals with cars and drivers in this town." It would be years before the board could convince him to purchase something more adequate.

CHOOSING THE BRIDGE TENDERS

Brian's first foray as a manager showed his inexperience. As the concept of C-SPAN began to take hold, he needed an assistant. Jana Fay, from the National Cable Television Association, applied. Prior to a lunch where the job would be offered, a friend tutored her on the questions to ask, especially those dealing with benefits. As usual, Brian wolfed down his lunch and asked Jana if she had any questions; she said, "What about benefits?" Brian responded, "What do you mean benefits?" Jana said, "You know, things like sick leave." Brian's simply responded, "I don't need sick leave, I never get sick," and went on from there with the issue never settled.

From the very beginning, Brian's job interviews are legendary, representing public affairs quizzes more than intelligence or skill assessment. "He cares less about what you think about issues or political personality than that you have gathered information and do think about such an issue." As one long-term staff member described it, "I entered Brian's bland office, done in shades of gray, and he began to lob questions at me in rapid-fire, 'What papers do you read? What columnist? What is their ideology?' It was intimidating, but his way of testing interest and awareness of public affairs." Another staff member explains that job interviews with Brian resemble a Journalism 101 template more than a traditional screening for employment. The questioning follows the pattern of "Who are You? Where are you from? What do you want to do?"

C-SPAN was not welcomed with open arms by the established media in Washington. Its young, nonunion staff seemed too eager to put in long hours. Technical staffs of the established media who might well be credited with establishing the "grunge look," were a bit disdainful of the C-SPAN staff with its Brian-enforced dress code. The established media were accustomed to zipping into a hearing, setting up the television lights to cover only the majority party members, and noisily packing their equipment after harvesting the initial sound bites.

MANAGEMENT BY TRIAL AND ERROR

At the outset, C-SPAN was an idea, not a business. "I never had a business course," Brian recalled recently. "I didn't know a thing about business. I had never run a business worth a dime. . . . I didn't know the difference between a profit or loss or any of that stuff. The only thing I brought to the table was an enormous desire; nothing else was that important." "It was unbelievable," one early board member remembered. "We'd come in here and go through the financials . . . and you'd ask questions that you'd ask at any level of business, a $50,000 or a $50 billion annual revenue business, and sometimes the eyes would glaze over. 'What did you want to know that for?'" These were good people, he said, but "there wasn't a lot of experience" at the network.

Everyone pitched in. Everyone has their story of sacrifice. When the corporate board came to Washington for a meeting, all hands, from Brian down, worked into the night to make sure the facilities were spotless. Bruce Collins, now Chief Counsel, remembers scrubbing the baseboards. Operations manager Brian Lockman points out that "Things were so tight that when you needed an extension cord, you brought one from home."[11] Most of the staff and certainly Brian view these examples as badges of honor. They became part of a founding story, emphasizing hard work, commitment, and personal sacrifice. They assumed that any complaint to Brian would be met with an icy, "You are a better person for it."

ONE MAN BAND

During the first few months on the air, Brian was "a one-man band" with a blindfold on. His commitment and sacrifices extended well beyond his staff in both scope and depth. He managed the day-to-day operations with limited help, smoothed conflicts with the House, and traveled around to affiliates making sure the technology was working. In his "spare" time, he was making plans for the future. All this was done from a one-person office in which three desks had been crammed and which could not receive the C-SPAN signal.

CHECKING THE TRAFFIC AND REDIRECTING THE FLOW

The addition of viewer call-ins came on a whim rather than emerging as part of a grand strategy. Sitting in the office in Arlington, Virginia, on Thanksgiving Day a few months after going on the air, Brian remembers saying, "You know, it would really be interesting to know whether anybody is watching this." A significant portion of Brian's vision included a two-way dialogue between the public and officials in Washington. In C-SPAN's early years, it was hard to know whether even the one-way on the bridge was working. C-SPAN could not be seen within the confines of the District of Columbia. If no one was watching, how could a dialogue develop?

No one had really considered talk-television. He had the technician on Capitol Hill flash up the number on the screen. "The minute the number came up on the screen, the phones started ringing off the hook." The setup was minimal, using three regular office phones at the National Press Club to talk to the chairman of the Federal Communications Commission. The whole enterprise almost bit the dust when the lights all blew out just before going on the air. Jan Fay remembers, "We took 40 calls within two minutes, and that's when we knew that there were people out there watching." For two hours, the phone lines lit up and a new venue for the public to bridge the Washington versus "flyover state" chasm emerged. From that first day, callers almost invariably thank C-SPAN and express their appreciation for the call-ins. "Thank God for C-SPAN" has almost replaced the more mundane "hello" when a call is answered. Callers often express as much pleasure to talk to C-SPAN as to confront the guest. After logging hundreds of hours behind the phones, Brian is impressed with "the extraordinary breadth of intelligence in the audience."

Brian continually showed a willingness to experiment. As one of the early staff members remembers, "Whenever Brian got frustrated, he would say, 'OK, we are going on the air.' It was almost therapy for him. He loved testing the pulse of the country through the call-ins." The move from Arlington, Virginia, to Capitol Hill was like "country kids going to the big city." It had been a miserable summer before the move with inadequate facilities and no air-conditioning.

Brian's personal needs were modest and he was generally willing to deal with what he was given by the board. On the other hand, when he believed in something, he was willing pursue it. Once he was convinced of the need for computers, he took up the cause against a board member who had no time for computers.

REFINING THE TWO-WAY BRIDGE

C-SPAN was and continues to be a work in progress. With some key exceptions, such as gavel-to-gavel House coverage, formats come and go. The decision to add call-in programs on television seemed like a stretch. Although

Larry King deserves credit for the first nationally broadcast radio call-in program, Brian initiated the first national television call-in in October 1980. With its demand for pictures, using television for a call-in raises the question of what would you do with a disembodied voice and an attentive host. Brian revels in the fact that among his callers, there are "people who know on every issue, more than the experts who live and work here [callers] who are experts on history, who have had firsthand experience in an industry in the middle of a debate can call up and say, 'I don't know what you are doing out there, but I've worked as an airplane pilot for the last 25 years, and you've just got it wrong.'"[12]

On the other hand, Brian recognizes that not all callers emerge with good information or the desire to participate in a reasoned discussion. Some of the callers are "aggressive people who have strong views and often strong negative views about everything . . . the more they talk, the better off it is. Let it rip, let people say what they want to say."[13]

PAYING THE TOLL

We often define ourselves by what we are not. Richard Nixon's famous phrase, "I am not a crook," could be seen as a simple statement of fact or as a temptation feared by both Nixon and his enemies. Brian's oft-repeated explanation of Washington politics in general and the media in particular, that one should "follow the money," seems to reflect his constant attempt to keep C-SPAN out of the money chase. Brian likes to point out that C-SPAN's $50 million budget for three networks, a dozen websites, and a radio channel is a fraction of the cost, for one year, of an hour program on CNN. He also practically gloats over the fact that the 5 cents per subscriber that C-SPAN receives from the cable industry has not been increased for years and pales in comparison to the continually escalating $2.90 per subscriber ESPN receives. He runs the entire C-SPAN network on a small percentage of what other cable networks spend on *one* of their regional offices. Brian holds out C-SPAN as one of the few institutions in Washington to which his generalization about money does not apply. He is proud of the fact that they do not measure ratings and don't have to worry about "counting eyeballs." Suggestions as to whether C-SPAN might use new technology or changed production techniques to increase audiences are met with an uncharacteristically abrupt and flat "no."

KEEPING THE BRIDGE OPEN

To some degree, C-SPAN became a victim of its own success. Initially, Brian cleverly sold his passion to cable owners arguing that by increasing value-added unique programming, such as C-SPAN, they could better sell cable subscriptions. As the available channel spots began to fill, operators looked for options to increase revenue. Once established, some cable operators saw an advantage in dumping C-SPAN in favor of networks willing to pay for time on the air. When some cable systems began dropping or limiting C-SPAN coverage, Brian felt a hatchet poised at his neck. While the funding agreement guaranteed C-SPAN's revenue stream, even from operators not using the signal, Brian's dream of national public affairs programming faced a challenge. As a passionate founder, Brian was willing to "take risks in desperate times." Rather than confronting the cable operators head-on, Brian orchestrated an oblique attack through the subscribers. Brian took to the air recommending that viewers call their cable company, thanking them for broadcasting C-SPAN and urging them to keep it on the air. The implied threat was subtle, but real. Not everyone was pleased. One representative from Cox Cable demanded that Brian get off the air. "Tell him to stop churning up cable systems across the country." As one cable executive put it, "I didn't take too kindly to this fellow we supported putting pressure on us. Who is this guy going around me and talking to my customers?" In the long run, viewer desires generally carried the day and most systems switched over to the new satellite that broadcasted C-SPAN.

MAINTAINING THE FLOW ON THE BRIDGE

Gavel-to-gavel coverage of House and Senate sessions, no matter how mundane or tedious, serve as the backbone of C-SPAN coverage and remain inviolate no matter what else is happening in the world. He responds to suggestions that C-SPAN might want to "cut back on some of the more boring stuff," with an old political saying that would immediately resonate with old patron Tip O'Neill. Brian reminds new C-SPAN staff that we "must dance with them that brung us." Brian feels strongly about his commitment to the chambers that "brung them" into the national consciousness.

Brian readily admits that putting Congress on the air was not his primary goal. The availability of the House signal was a vehicle for his primary desire to open up the media mix and provide more choice. If the initiative had stopped there, Brian's goals would not have been met to any significant degree. C-SPAN was one among many of his thrusts against the big three networks that started with cable and has continued with the Internet.

EXPANDING THE TRAFFIC PATTERN

Brian always envisioned a broad definition of public affairs. He longed for C-SPAN cameras in committee rooms, meeting halls, and other public places where the public's work was being done. He insisted that decisions of what to cover be based on objective criteria related to the importance of the issue and a commitment to balance perspectives. He established a rotating in-house "shoot" committee of which he was not a part. At first, their choices were relatively limited as both governmental and private policy forums either refused to allow their cameras or simply failed to inform them of upcoming events. As C-SPAN became the "network of record," the volume of option expanded.

We are all creatures of our own backgrounds and interests. A key connecting rod in C-SPAN's ability to objectively bridge the world of public affairs and the public is the daily shoot committee meeting, where decisions on which events C-SPAN cameras will cover are made. Every day, there are dozens of committee hearings, speeches, press conferences, and policy seminars. Coverage of the House and the Senate are givens. Beyond that, there is an attempt to balance policy realms, regional considerations, and ideological positions. Grandfather and C-SPAN consultant John Splaine tells of sitting on a shoot meeting and having his interest piqued by an upcoming Congressional hearing on grandparents' rights. "It was a big issue to me, but no interest to board members since none were part of the population affected." The decision to skip the hearing was no surprise for a group of thirty-somethings. With a staff that is relatively well-off financially, limited in the number of minorities, relatively well educated, they tend to choose issues of relevance to their interests.

A POTENTIAL BUMP IN THE ROAD

Brian promised to bring the House to the public, warts and all. Throughout history, individuals have gained advantage by being the first to use new technology to advantage. In politics, we remember Franklin Roosevelt's masterful use of radio and John Kennedy's skill with television. New technologies are often tools for the disadvantaged to gain more equal footing with contemporary power holders. While the Democrats controlled the cameras in the House, Brian's commitment to cover the House gavel-to-gavel came back to bite Speaker Tip O'Neill and his Democratic colleagues. During the early 1980s, a group of hot-headed, young Republicans, calling themselves the Conservative Opportunity Society, availed themselves of the House rules and Brian's commitment to present a coordinated set of speeches at the end of the legislative day during a period called "special orders." Speaking to a largely empty chamber, they excoriated the Democratic leadership and the policies they supported. Their words became magnified as they encouraged their supporters to watch C-SPAN and as the media took up their drum roll.

O'Neill and company were not happy. Some CEOs would be hesitant to bite the hand that feeds them, but Brian avoided the temptation to declare special orders as after-the-gavel shenanigans. O'Neill decided to take things in his own hands and quell the gnats through embarrassment. Without warning to the current speaker Robert Walker (R-Penn.), O'Neill ordered the cameras to span the empty chamber. When informed of the changed procedures, Walker used it as another example of high-handed Democratic tactics. The next day, O'Neill took the extraordinary step for a Speaker, and took to the floor to personally criticize the Republican orators. The extremity of his criticism led to a call to have the Speaker's words "taken down." Standing on the floor, O'Neill suffered the embarrassment of having his comments struck from the *Congressional Record* as if they had never been spoken. The so-called "CAMSCAM" flap helped create much wider awareness to C-SPAN. One of O'Neill's staff indicated that O'Neill's rebuke helped solidify his retirement plans, recognizing that "politics is just not what it used to be." He later confided privately that allowing himself to be talked into the cameras by Brian and others was, "the worst damn fool mistake I ever made."

BUILDING THE SECOND BRIDGE LANE

Senator Robert Byrd (D-WV) was unwilling to venture out until he knew where the votes were. As a party leader, he was accustomed to counting votes. C-SPAN had been regularly polling senators on their openness to television coverage as part of their campaign to complement their House coverage. Over the years, the arrival of a younger generation of Senators more comfortable before the camera had swelled the support to sixty-two solid commitments. Senator Byrd called Brian and Mike Michaelson to his office and asked only one question, "Are these vote figures solid?"

A couple of hitches remained. The memory of the recent CAM-SCAM scandal made some senators wary of how their actions might be portrayed on the floor. On the personal level, Byrd was torn. He loves the Senate, has spent the majority of his life within its chambers, and serves as its unofficial historian. He recognized that without public visibility, the Senate could become a second-class legislative body in the eyes of the public. Byrd is also worried about his personal legacy. Brian had laid down the gauntlet, the commitment to gavel-to-gavel coverage. Byrd was not only worried about boring the public, but also being seen as nothing but a "me, too" leader. Republican leader Howard Baker (R-TN) had bought into the gavel-to-gavel approach, but was never able to muster the necessary votes. Eventually, Byrd dropped his plans to limit coverage and Brian's "fly on the wall," gavel-to-gavel approach prevailed.

With an idea of where he stood, Byrd went about building the necessary coalition to pass the legislation. Under Senate rules, he knew that simply having a majority may not be enough. The right of unlimited debate (the filibuster) and other delaying tactics allows one senator to tie up the entire chamber. As Senator Simpson described the Senate process, "One person can tie this place in a knot. And two can do it even more beautifully."[14] In building coalitions in Congress, one hopes to convert opponents into supporters and thus have a net gain of two votes (denying the opposition one and gaining one for your side). Such a dramatic conversion is often difficult. An alternative strategy lies in toning down the opposition and getting a commitment that the opponent will not use all the strategies available. Recognizing the realities of coalition building and the potential problem of delaying tactics, Senator Byrd pinpointed Senator Russell Long (D-LA) as a key stumbling block to Senate television. After Senator Byrd (D-WV) became convinced that television should be allowed, he met with Long and recalled telling Senator Long: "Russell, you and I are not going to be around here always. . . . Television is coming to the Senate . . . the American people are entitled to see us at our work . . . the Senate . . . is rapidly becoming the invisible force. The House is seen on C-SPAN. Everybody knows what the House is doing. Why shouldn't they see the Senate, in which senators speak longer and in greater depth about the subject matter? . . . So, Russell, why don't you and I work to bring this about while we're here?" So, Russell Long was persuaded. He never was persuaded to vote for it, but his opposition to it lessened considerably, and it made it possible for television to come to the Senate.[15]

AN ESTABLISHED PUBLIC UTILITY

Brian is hesitant about either touting his own success or diminishing that of others. When asked about Newton Minnow's (chairman of the Federal Communications Commission) speech calling television programming a "vast wasteland," Brian showed charity. "I think [Newton Minow] was right about an enormous amount of television, but I think you could say that about an enormous amount of things American. One person's wasteland is another person's great pleasure."[16]

6

BRIDGE MAINTENANCE
Management by Walking Around

All truly great thoughts are conceived by walking.

—Friedrich Nietzsche (1844–1900)

While Brian Lamb eschews creating a leadership model for others, he follows a series of principles that would serve most would-be leaders well. First, he wears the mantle of leadership lightly, encouraging employees to call him by his first name. Second, he hires people he has "a great deal of confidence in to do the job and leave[s] them alone." Third, he manages "by walking around," getting to know his employees both personally and in relation to their professional challenges.

Brian exhibits a strong sense of loyalty to his friends, staff, supporters, and early vendors. He treats his staff like family, playing the role of mother hen. He knows who's pregnant, whose kids are in trouble, and who is sick. In any kind of personal challenge or tragedy, he is the first to call and stands ready to do anything he can. No one is surprised when he shows up at the hospital or knows more about a staff member's need than his or her supervisor. Staff members are convinced, "This is not a gimmick. Brian is truly interested. His concern for people is part of his inherent DNA."

Brian's management by walking around is probably the most unique characteristic. A look at his daily appointment book is deceiving. He roams the halls, addressing everyone by their first name, treating everyone equally. Brian recognizes that "people would rather talk to you in their space than in yours."[1] He estimates that 20 percent of his time is spent intentionally wandering the halls. Encountering Brian in the hallway can intimidate some newer employees, fearful that he is checking to see whether or not they are doing their job.

Brian's legendary walks around the halls emerge not from a need to check up on people, but rather to find out about them and their jobs. He is the "information antenna" of the organization, gathering information directly from the source, reducing the need for formal channels. A walk around the halls with Brian includes a mix of personal questions and business. A good dose of teasing helps open people up. Humorous nicknames set the tone.

Hallway conversations are not typical bull sessions. Brian is like "a collegial headmaster, chatty and amiable, yet demanding objectivity from coworkers even when they talk politics by the water cooler."[2] When guests confront him in the hallway, he becomes the master of ceremonies, introducing them to the staff and others. It takes only a few moments of following him to recognize he is interested in those who work at C-SPAN and in what they have to say. Talks range from family, to trips on the C-SPAN bus, to a recent program seen or a book read. Interns first meet him with an "oh, yeah" look when he tells them "call me Brian." That look turns to incredulity when in the midst of his talk with them, Teresa Easley, a Human Resources assistant, pokes her head in the door and says "That's Brian, don't go to lunch with him."

Brian's lunches are an institution at C-SPAN. Started in response to the possibility of a strike in the early 1980s, they are yet another way to check the pulse of the network and to involve those in the organization. Brian is known as the world's fastest eater, allowing him plenty of time to engage in conversation. The lunch is the excuse; exchanging information is the purpose. "The talk" is open, free, and wide-ranging, albeit somewhat intimidating to newer employees who are still learning the C-SPAN way.

HOME BASE

A person's office tells you a great deal about their interests, hopes, and desires. When C-SPAN moved into its present location, Brian eschewed choosing the corner office with its dramatic view of Capitol Hill, instead choosing the side with the ability to observe the street and giving him an oblique view of Union Station, where he had spent so many hours as a young lieutenant. Stepping into Brian's office, "you feel as though you've entered someone's private library. The walls are lined with hundreds of books."[3] The physical arrangement reflects his nonauthoritarian approach. Rather than having a large, power-symbol desk between "lowly petitioners" and "the boss," Brian created an open office, with one desk facing the window and a round table where guests can meet on equal ground. His self-confidence comes out in his view that "I've got the job with the title. . . . I don't need to constantly reinforce it."

Although not the intention, Brian's view of the street allows him the ability to catch his employees standing in line for cappuccino from a street vendor. Bothered by the extended coffee breaks this represented, Brian approached the problem indirectly. Rather than throwing a fit or firing off a nasty memo, he simply purchased an upscale cappuccino machine for the break room, drawing his employees back into the building and back into a more reasonable coffee break period.

From the very beginning, Brian established an open-door policy for his staff. "The lowest of low can walk into the CEO's office for a chat."

A VIEW FROM THE BRIDGE DECK

Some bridge tenders seek the broad view, looking over the grand sweep of their responsibilities. Others walk the bridge deck looking for loose bolts and trash that might cause accidents. Brian's approach falls into the latter category. His office is more of a home base than an executive throne room, where employees are called in for good or bad news. He hardly ever seems too busy to chat.[4] While the staff joke about the executive offices as "mahogany row," the very fact that it is a joke tells a great deal about the relative egalitarianism promoted.

Brian's management by walking around provides an almost family atmosphere at C-SPAN. Brian knows his employee's spouses and children. His staff recognizes that "he wants to know everybody like they are a nephew or a niece and, in turn, expects the same kind of interest." Seeing Brian come down the hall is not always an unmixed blessing. He uses his staff as a way to sample the American public about their level of knowledge. He is just as likely to ask, "How is Ashley's soccer team doing?" as "Can you tell me where Bosnia is?" It is not that he does not know, but rather he is testing what one might expect of the relatively well-educated and informed C-SPAN audience. When only one of nine staff members gathered around the water cooler could place Bosnia, he knew how difficult it was going to be to explain the story.

The lengths Brian goes to in support of his staff permeate the halls of C-SPAN, but are much more than public relations gimmicks. He really cares. When a relatively new staff member's baby died of SIDS out of state, Brian gathered a couple of key staff members and immediately traveled to the site to show his concern.

Brian explains, "In this leadership business, you can spew a lot of clichés. It is very easy to have a great deal of theory. But I've found that the more ownership someone can take, the more likely they're going to do a superb job."[5]

FILLING CRACKS IN THE BRIDGE

Brian never imagined that C-SPAN would grow to its present size and become as institutionalized as it is. He always saw it as a family. He never wanted to lay anyone off. He had to bring on others to deal with areas outside his comfort zone. Brian is a visionary, promoter, inspirer, and master interviewer—not a bad toolbox of skills. He is not a personnel or budget manager. The C-SPAN board of directors recognized this and sent him help to put C-SPAN on a firmer business footing. To his credit, Brian accepted help without protest, thus freeing him from the conflict that he hated and allowing him to do those things he loves. Few leaders can do it all, and Brian proves the advantage of giving up those things at which you do not excel.

The first major addition was Mike Michaelson, the former head of the House and Radio Television Gallery. While his job was to oversee the day-to-day operations of the network, his forte lay more in using his contacts on Capitol Hill to solve problems and smooth relations with friends he had made after thirty years on the Hill. In the loose organizational approach favored by Brian, Bruce Collins, a young staffer with the National Cable Television Association was brought in as director of network operations. Unfortunately, or perhaps intentionally, Brian never communicated Collins' expected role and as one staff member put it, "Everyone continued to run around doing everything and anything."

In 1985, Paul FitzPatrick arrived as chief operating officer, charged with moving C-SPAN from a small mom-and-pop organization run out of Brian's hip pocket to a modern corporation with clear lines of authority, specific job descriptions, fixed financial routines, and established personnel policies. To a large degree, Brian retained the "mom" of the operation, contributing the passion, loyalty, and personal concern, while FitzPatrick was the stern "pop" insisting on routinized and inflexible rules. Brian stepped back and allowed FitzPatrick to create structure, while he retained the spirit of the place.

Weaning himself from being the all-encompassing decision maker was not seamless. One of the early employees still on the staff points out that "especially during the first five years, we had a real tie with Brian and wanted to do what Brian wanted. He was that father figure." It was difficult to recognize the rights of others to have the final say about things. With the founding father in the hallway, it is natural for all the staff to seek his approval. Key staff members admit thinking about products or decisions, "Did Brian like it? Did Brian approve? Shouldn't Brian know about this?"

Despite the bottom-up mantra of idea generation, Brian admits, "I come up with a lot of ideas, but the real difference probably is that I don't dictate that they use them." It is a give and take, where Brian encourages his staff to refine or reject ideas. Then he steps back and gives a great deal of freedom in carrying out the plan. In Brian's words, "The one thing that I have learned is, you can't hover. People don't like that. . . . I believe strongly in letting people do their thing." Inevitably, staff members whose ideas win out praise the system, while others harbor feelings of favoritism. The desire to please Brian can lead to a single-minded focus, missing broader and more important issues. For the 1997 nonelection year programming focus, Brian had fully endorsed programs following the 1831 travels of Baron de Tocqueville. On the day Senator Robert Dole (R-KS) was to announce his decision to resign from the Senate to spend full time on his presidential campaign, the C-SPAN program staff had planned a large meeting to discuss plans for the Tocqueville series, giving short shrift to Dole's historical decision. Coverage of the announcement went on with a rookie producer and the quality of the production showed it.

In many organizations, ideas are vetted through many layers of decision making. While C-SPAN is open to ideas from many corners, Brian's "vote" counts more than others. If he has an idea and no one can uncover its fatal flaw, it becomes policy. The seed for the C-SPAN bus was planted when Sarah Trahern convinced Brian to invite Doug Brinkley, author of *The Magic Bus*, to appear on *Booknotes*. To better teach American history and literature, Brinkley had taken a busload of students across the country to see historical sites and meet literary figures. Brian was taken with the idea. Once he had talked with the author, the C-SPAN bus was born. It travels around the country with C-SPAN staff visiting schools, providing another kind of bridge with Washington.

Brian seems smart enough to know that he could never serve as the autocratic boss who scares unwavering compliance out of his "minions." He treats his entire staff with respect, and laughs at the fact that his top-level colleagues make fun of him to his face. He admits that "they have to endure my stories." Brian jokes that the two executives "live for the day" when he comes up with a new story.[6] Loyalty begets loyalty. C-SPAN's turnover remains low. The first cameraman and secretary remain on the payroll, albeit in elevated jobs. Staff expansion has guaranteed Brian the position of "senior citizen in C-SPAN's . . . thirty-something hierarchy."[7] Brian practices management with the human touch. As Jana Fay, his most senior employee puts it, "This is a great place to work. Brian always wants his employees to learn and tells them, 'If you are not having fun, you shouldn't be here.' Brian has always been very loyal to people, especially to those loyal to him by staying around."

In the early years, no detail went beyond Brian's attention. When a staff member removed a doorstop that had become a danger for walkers, Brian was quick to observe the indentation in the carpet and ask, "What happened here?" The question served as less of a condemnation than a curiosity. The explanation was enough to counter the possible reaction, "Why didn't you get approval?"

While correcting one's subordinates can take on the character of going to the woodshed, Brian's quiet demeanor and honest concern make him come across more as a concerned schoolmaster. Whether he explicitly says it or not, the message to someone mispronouncing a word or misusing a fact comes across as, "I don't want you to embarrass yourself."

Brian's staff remembers, "He is still a public relations man and knows how to make a positive impact. For C-SPAN's first major Christmas party in 1984, he eschewed the poster on the wall or Xeroxed invitation. He invited every staff member to his office to personally tell them about the time, place, and details. It was like a little political campaign that made everyone feel important."

ONE MAN'S BRIDGE IS ANOTHER'S DETOUR

Not everyone appreciates the highly personal nature of C-SPAN decision making, dominated by the quirks and fascinations of Brian. The perceived need to invent programming during nonelection years encouraged C-SPAN to push the envelope on what is defined as public affairs. Year-long forays into the travels of Alexis de Toqueville, the encouragement of reenactments of the Lincoln-Douglas debates, and a series on American presidents with a prominent place for showing their gravesites were seen by some as squandering resources, not contemporary themes of greater relevance.

Brian (second from left) participated in sports vicariously as high school team manager. C-SPAN archives

Brian's boyhood passion turns into his first regular job at WASK.
C-SPAN archives

Brian and WASK owner Henry Rosenthal in the mobile studio.
C-SPAN archives

Brian hones his interviewing skills on "Dance Date," his creation and entrée into the media.
C-SPAN archives

Lieutenant Lamb, reporting for duty.
C-SPAN archives

Brian tours his parents around Capitol Hill, little expecting it would dominate the rest of his life.
C-SPAN archives

Brian expresses his mock frustration with the hearing process that slowed down the building of the C-SPAN transmission station.
C-SPAN archives

PUBLIC HEARING
FAIRFAX COUNTY

ON **BOARD OF ZONING APPEALS** F
DATE JAN 9, 79   11:10 AM
VARIANCE V-300-78
SHELL OIL CO. & NAT. CABLE SATELLITE CORP.
TO ALLOW ERECTION OF 100' TOWER 13' FROM
PROP. LINE OF REAR YARD (60' SETBACK
APPROX. 700'S TO REAR OF SIGN

RD ROOM, A' LEVEL
SSEY BUILDING
CHAIN BRIDGE ROAD
FAIRFAX, VA.
L 691-2381
NOT BE REMOVED OR
ER PENALTY OF LAW.

Brian meets with House Speaker Thomas "Tip" O'Neill and his staff about covering the House.
C-SPAN archives

Brian (right) presides over the first C-SPAN call-in.
C-SPAN archives

Brian and Paul Fitzpatrick meet Senator Robert Byrd (D-WV) in the C-SPAN control booth on the first day of Senate coverage.
C-SPAN archives

Uncomfortable with learning second hand, Brian visits one of the sites of the Lincoln-Douglas debates.
C-SPAN archives

A spoof painting hanging in the C-SPAN archives portraying what it might have looked like if Brian had interviewed Abraham Lincoln.
C-SPAN archives

Brian's hand-picked and molded successors, Rob Kennedy and Susan Swain.
C-SPAN archives

Brian's brother, Jim, visits the old bicycle bridge that played such a role in Brian's life.
Stephen E. Frantzich

George W. Bush awards Brian the Presidential Medal of Freedom.
Alex Wong / Getty Images News

FAIR ACCESS TO THE BRIDGE

Schooled in the values of fair play and justice, Brian's personal goal for C-SPAN has nothing to do with promoting particular politicians, parties, or policies. As he puts it, "I thought from the very beginning that this was going to create a more level playing field in this town for all points of view. And this network would create an opportunity to listen to the extremes on the left and the right. I think it is very important when you're trying to have a debate in the political system like ours, that you get away from just the middle, the establishment, and let the public decide on their own what their views are."[8]

We are often challenged to face up to the assertion: "If we are not part of the solution, we are part of the problem." When C-SPAN's balance during call-ins came into question, the decision was made to label the telephone lines as "for the president" and "against the president," or "for the Republicans" and "for the Democrats." The decision allowed hosts to switch back and forth and present an image of fairness. Observers expressed two related concerns. On the one hand, the equal switching back and forth implies that each side has equal support in the population. Second, labeling people first and listening to their ideas second diminishes the impact of the arguments and encourages listeners to store up ammunition from "their side in the issue." In their view, such an approach simply mimics the national media, contributes to partisanship, and limits thoughtful discussion.

NOBODY'S PERFECT: THE DANGER
OF THE BRIDGE BREAKING DOWN

Personal strengths and weaknesses often emerge as two sides of the same coin. Everyone thinks they want a boss who exudes personal concern, humor, and a pleasant demeanor. Organizationally, other characteristics are often needed. Brian's "Midwestern nice," engenders some limitations. He has a hard time delivering bad news. More comfortable with the "good guy" rather than the "bad guy" role, he foists firings and severe criticisms on others. Those tasked with dealing with bad news recognize that Brian is "just wired in a way that can't hurt people."

Praise and criticism seldom explode in animated form from Brian. Stories of him screaming and yelling about anything are virtually nonexistent. He does get frustrated with things like equipment malfunctions, mispronounced names, and missed opportunities. His approach to criticism revolves around tempering the sting by revealing his own shortcomings and trying to make the process into a learning experience. He might casually catch a host in the hallway and say, "You know, I used to mispronounce that name myself, but I believe it should be pronounced _____," or " I know it is hard to skim all the papers in the morning, but it is important to catch those that deal with _____."

Brian works long and hard on the projects he enjoys. His mastery of project avoidance for those activities he finds less palatable leads to a little tug-of-war as staff attempt to get things to the top of his pile and he works on the premise that if he avoids the task long enough, it will go away. In recent years, the issue is less critical since Brian is not directly involved in the day-to-day operation of the network. He now deals with the big, long-term issues and serves as the network spokesman to the cable industry and the public. It is a far cry from the early years when he pulled cables and built sets.

It is one thing to have limitations. It is another to ignore or fail to admit them. Brian is willing to build on his manifold areas of strength and leave areas of weakness to others. His passionate commitment to C-SPAN overwhelms the need to serve as all-encompassing infielder.

The luxury of organizational growth and Brian's recognition of his own strengths and weaknesses resulted in a division of labor. It is a far cry from the early years when Brian had to do it all.

A DAY IN THE LIFE

The shifts from junior officer in the Navy, to congressional staff person, to reporter, and now to chief executive has done little to change Brian's personal routine. He still gets up at 4:00 AM, gets his coffee fix, and devours a number of newspapers and other reading material. For most of his career, dinner meant fast food at the Pentagon metro food court. Those envisioning Brian in the midst of Washington power dinners or power lunches would be sorely disappointed. Brian's commitment to C-SPAN is pervasive. More than one close friend said, "He is married to C-SPAN" or "C-SPAN is his mistress." While others were raising families of pursuing hobbies in their spare time, "He thinks about it seven days a week." In C-SPAN consultant John Splaine's words, "Brian does a wonderful job of making a family out of C-SPAN, both for himself and his employees."

DETOURS AND SPEED BUMPS

Brian shepherded C-SPAN through four union challenges. All emerged from the field crews, but had the potential to include much of the staff. With cameramen heavily unionized in most settings, it was inevitable that professional colleagues would talk while working in the field. The field staff brought back dreams of more benefits and union protection. While Brian comes across as calm and unflappable, his closest associates recognize that he is "hyper-sensitive" to criticism.

One of the events that most hurt Brian was the attempt to unionize. Brian and most of the C-SPAN staff saw the operation as a small family place, where the constraints of union rules would threaten its existence. C-SPAN ran on a "whatever is needed, I will do" atmosphere, rather than working to a union contract. Brian could not understand others who lacked his commitment to C-SPAN and its extraordinary demands.

After the 1984 presidential campaign coverage strained the human and economic resources of C-SPAN, there was a great letdown when post-election demands did not decline. Poor equipment, modest salaries, and long hours all took their toll. Brian took the initial push for unionization very personally as a referendum on his leadership and a threat to C-SPAN's very existence. He saw the organizers as disloyal. Brian fought the initiative on two fronts. He talked with every member of the bargaining unit that was concentrated among the field staff, approaching it like a political campaign soliciting concerns and asking for "no" votes. He also went back to the cable industry, indicating the need to treat C-SPAN like a real business rather than an experimental project. Part of the commitment he received from the cable industry was a one cent per subscriber rate increase to provide the resources needed to satisfy some of the personnel concerns.

The pressure for unionization did raise some legitimate issues, largely associated with communications and not having enough attention paid to individuals. Brian admitted, "We screwed up and won't do it again. Give us another chance." He instituted a number of one-on-one meetings to dissuade support for the union. In the eventual vote, the union lost 12 to 24, but considerable repair work remained. Brian saw it was a "huge vote of confidence." Following his pattern of trying to learn from all experiences, new initiatives to improve personal communications emerged. Brian began a "Lunch with Brian" program, providing employees an outlet for their concerns aimed at the highest level of management.

Two subsequent attempts to unionize fizzled. In 2006, the issue arose again. Brian stepped back and allowed his two successors, Rob Kennedy and Susan Swain, to take the lead since "they would be the ones dealing with the consequences." Brian advised and guided, only pushing hard not to hire a group of "beat the union" consultants. After extensive meetings, both individually and with groups, the union lost 29 to 4, validating Brian's goal of "not keeping unions out, but keeping C-SPAN together." Just as in 1985, one of the results was to formalize communications. The Brian Lamb "listening lunches" found supplements in the Kennedy/Swain listening lunches and dinners.

WE "DON'T GET NO RESPECT"

As C-SPAN's creator, manager, and cheerleader, Brian was often forced to recognize that other media and political institutions expressed little esteem for what they were doing.

Mike Michaelson, C-SPAN Executive Vice President, remembers that camera crews would come back filled with frustration after confrontations with network crews who challenged the "new kids on the block trying to sabotage coverage by invoking union rules and intimidating young C-SPAN technicians. They didn't think we were a bonafide news organization."

Over a dozen years into C-SPAN's existence, the problem of legitimacy continued. For example, prior to the 1992 national nominating conventions, organizers inadvertently left C-SPAN representatives out of several important planning sessions. The workspace given the network was poor. Master control was assigned to an area that suffered power failures. To add insult to injury, Brian was among a number of journalists who exited the convention hall the first night only to find his car towed "from a lot the police had instructed them to park in." To make matters worse, the officers could not tell Brian to which of three possible locations his car had been taken. He found it in a lot ten miles away. Cab fares and fines hit the three-figure mark. It should have been a good week for Brian. There was "a whole page in *Time* magazine devoted to him," as well as "high marks from *The Los Angeles Times*." Brian, however, dislikes personal attention. The final blow came on a call-in program he hosted when a female viewer accused the network of favoring the Democrats. Bias is the only charge a viewer can make which lets them know the usually complacent network head has a pulse. Brian had had enough and left Houston early.

DON'T DIS THE BRIDGE BUILDER

Brian consistently reaches out, encouraging others to use the bridge. His soft spot for education resulted in significant C-SPAN resources committed to educators who might promote the link to information only C-SPAN provides. For over a decade, C-SPAN hosted hundreds of college professors in three-day Seminars for Professors, with the goal of familiarizing them with the uses of C-SPAN in the classroom. C-SPAN picked up all the costs, once the faculty members arrived in Washington. The program came under increasing scrutiny, not because of its positive impact on participants, but rather whether the time and effort might better be spent on the high school level, where it would be more visible to cable operators. The program might have gone on if one person had not angered Brian. At the final dinner for one of the seminars, a faculty member cornered Brian and berated him over C-SPAN's lack of diversity. Brian believed that C-SPAN's staff and programming reflected society well. To add insult to injury, the faculty member carried over his criticism to the public question-and-answer session with Brian after the dinner. It was "the straw that broke the camel's back." Brian was polite, but told his staff, "That was like inviting someone to your home and them insulting you in front of your guests." The death knell for the Seminar for Professors rang.

A LINK TO THE POWERS THAT BE

Brian ultimately remains C-SPAN's link to the cable industry through C-SPAN's board of directors. Without the cable industry, C-SPAN's programming content would have no public outlet. He must walk a fine line between ceding control to the board and keeping them impotent and, therefore, illegitimate in the eyes of their business colleagues. Brian's line in the sand emerged over programming content. If the cable industry or any political faction were to dictate programming content, the entire rationale of C-SPAN as an objective vehicle for reporting on politics would go by the wayside. With programming content off the table, the board could play an important and legitimate role in improving financial practices, personnel policies, and programming formats.

Brian gives a great deal of credit to his board of directors, as the "real heroes of this place." While supportive, the board can also be exasperating. Sitting around a table with a lot of self-made millionaires guarantees the presence of some strong egos and frustration with being rubber stamps.

Although major C-SPAN expenditures are rounding errors on the budgets these cable operators deal with every day, their sharp pencils would emerge. Brian says, "I used to sit at these board meetings and say, 'I can't believe you're fussing over this little stuff, when you guys are dealing in the mega-millions.' But they could understand it. After you get up to the mega-zeros, people think it's another zero."[9] The board generally has little to worry about. When it comes to spending money, Brian is "very parsimonious. He was taught in early years the value of money." The corporate culture reflects "its founder's contempt for pomp and excess. He doesn't spend money he does not have, and doesn't make commitments he cannot honor."[10] From the beginning, Brian saved money by hiring part-time employees, tested out new hires with two-week trial runs, and never sought a salary increase for himself. There was never any question about getting one's value out of Brian. As Tom Wheeler, former president of the national Cable Television Association recalled, Brian "lived, ate, and breathed C-SPAN. If ever there was total dedication, Lamb had it."[11]

7

MANAGING THE FLOW
The Lamb Style

If your mouth is open, you are not learning anything.

—Brian Lamb

UOB: THE UNIVERSITY OF BRIAN

To be honest, Brian could not imagine anything named after him, particularly a university. He would be only a little less appalled with a blue-collar type of name, such as "BS" (Brian State). His less than stellar record in academic settings obscures the fact that he loves to learn. In some ways, C-SPAN allows him to live his fantasy of constantly learning in the "University of the Real World," with the best professors around, those individuals who are directly involved in public affairs on a day-to-day basis. Brian is quick to admit that "My reason to get into C-SPAN was fairly selfish; I wanted an alternative on my television set." He once told a reporter, "Listen, I'm a classic 'C' student from Purdue University in Lafayette, Indiana. . . . I'm not a brain surgeon. If you watch it, you can figure it out."[1] Brian is quick to admit that he was "not much of a booker in those days." He explains, with no rancor or blame, "My parents weren't book readers. They never played classical music in the house. They encouraged education, but did not have a clear idea that it was so important."

Brian was picky and choosy about what he learned in school. Latin and chemistry stood out as neither his best nor favorite subjects. It showed. His Latin grades were so bad that the Latin teacher had to tutor him. Years later, after seeing him on the air, Miss Carolyn Griffin wrote him a "you probably don't remember me" letter. Brian shot back good-naturedly, "Not only do I remember you, but you gave me an 'F'." She protested his memory and sent her 40-year-old grade book to him clearly showing a 'D.' Confident in his own value, Brian proudly keeps the grade book on his desk. Brian is quick to point out to anyone in hearing distance that "My number on goal was not getting 'A's"—and I proved it. . . . I was a 'C' student. If you're not interested in learning, it doesn't work. As I grew older and wanted to learn and desperately wanted inside information, learning was a lot easier."[2]

WHICH LANE IS HE IN?

A continuous guessing game, both inside C-SPAN and without, involves guessing Brian's personal political affinity. Any indication of political preference expressed verbally or nonverbally in his fiefdom remains out of order. So good are Brian's reactions that one caller addressed his comments calling him "Ol' Great Poker Face!" The host's job in Brian's view is to help inform the people and the people to inform their guests.

Individuals passionate about government and politics are usually passionate about encouraging government to do or not do something. Brian's passion baffles most political junkies. He literally pounds his fist on the desk when he explains, "I am truly politically neutral. I would never be a member of a political party. I really don't care who wins." His commitment lies in opening up the system, helping to ensure that both the eventual winners and losers have a chance to make their case in an unfettered way. After one group wins, his attention turns to allowing the public to look over their shoulders to see if they live up to their commitments.

Brian's reputation for fairness and nonpartisanship belie his background. At first glance, one might assume that someone who had worked in the Nixon administration and for a Republican Senator from Colorado would wear his political allegiance on his sleeve and promote it whenever he had a chance. Nevertheless, he is proud of and a true believer in the C-SPAN staff dictum, "If you care who wins, you should not be working here" which one almost expects to be chiseled on the walls of the corporate offices. The sign is invisible, but just as real. He explains the seeming inconsistency by saying that during his years of political work, "I never committed to anyone. . . . The more I was in it, the more I knew I just did not belong."[3] It is not so much that he does not have strong personal views, but that his commitment to open government and unbiased news coverage supersedes his personal political goals. His personal accommodation with being an outsider unexpectedly allows a greater portion of the American public to see the process from the inside.

Keeping his own political leanings to himself, Brian asks his staff to check their political preferences at the door. "Just when everyone in journalism has agreed that objectivity is a snare and a delusion, Brian refuses to convey the slightest hint of his own views, even over whether he has any."[4] Even those who interact with him up close have difficulty categorizing him. During a call in show, Senator John McCain (R-AZ) quipped that in his best judgment, "I think he is a vegetarian." Brian would not be unhappy with such a nonanswer. As one observer put it, "In fact, C-Span is so neutral, you'd have to slice founder Brian Lamb down the middle to find out if he's a Republican or Democrat."[5]

Brian's commitment to objectivity and serenity usually overwhelms his own ego and feelings. However, even Brian is human. During a call-in at the 1992 Republican Convention in Houston, Brian fielded a call from a woman complaining that she had been seeing and hearing too many Republicans. Brian remembers that "She really teed me off, and I teed right back." He suggested that if she did not like what she was seeing she might consider changing channels. Pretty tame stuff for most call-in hosts, but the uncharacteristic "outburst" bothered Brian. Since no one in house was going to question his performance, Brian did himself, leaving the convention, assigning others to cover his portions of the program, and accepting a "time out" for two weeks.[6]

Perhaps Brian is on to something. Not everyone wants to know what everyone else thinks. A long-time fan of the network, taking a tour of the facilities, met Brian in the hallway. After expressing that it was the best part of the tour, she said, "We still don't know what you think." "Good," Brian responded. And she replied, "I don't want to know." As he headed back to his office, Brian said, "That is the best thing they can ever say to you."[7]

THE PUBLIC FACE: FAR FROM THE FAST LANE

Brian has virtually created a public persona by avoiding public persona status. He prides himself on his bland low-key approach and, yes, his lack of star quality. He readily admits, "I don't want any charisma. It's not my goal."[8] He has been described as a "cultural white board," with no political bias, but rather "a screen for ideological projection" of others' ideas.[9]

As one publication pointed out, "You know, the nice, plain fellow who runs C-SPAN. He's the network's chairman and chief executive officer, and comes across like John Doe. Think of the opposite of Sam Donaldson and you've got Brian Lamb."[10]

KEEPING THE LANES OPEN

While it is often hard to determine Brian's political views, there is one issue on which he is passionate. He cannot stand censorship. "He gets ticked off when he finds something that has been censored." In preparation for the Lincoln-Douglas debates, he became aware of the fact that Lincoln's words at Charleston had often been cut because of what some saw as a racial slur. Brian included a statement in the letter to participating communities that the persons portraying Lincoln and Douglas must present the full speeches without editing or censorship.

If censorship in the abstract rankles Brian, efforts directed at his network remain even less palatable. When a C-SPAN camera crew arrived late for a tour of Walter Reed Medical Center during the 2007 flap over the care of veterans, Walter Reed's chief spokesperson refused to let them in arguing they were "not on the list." The next day, Brian went on the air with emotion seldom seen on his face and asked, "What kind of public relations organization would want to withhold, in our case, a network that showed his entire tour?"[11]

Brian is not afraid to show his own ignorance or intervene on behalf of the audience, which might not be aware of an event or a term. At times, Brian's directness throws interview subjects off their stride. When Winston Churchill biographer Martin Gilbert slipped in the comment that Churchill had been charged with "buggery," Brian jumped in and asked for a definition. When Gilbert tried to reverse the question asking, "You don't know what buggery is?" Brian shot back with another request for a definition. Gilbert flailed around finally saying it was a euphemism for "an unnatural act of the Oscar Wilde type," still not able to give a clear definition, but providing the audience with enough information to make sense of the earlier comments. Brian explains his inquiring from the fact that "my curiosity level is higher than most people, but I am really of average intellect and average knowledge, and so when I ask a question, I am asking it for the average person."[12]

Brian's assumption remains simple. "I start out with the premise that everyone has a fascinating story to tell. My job is to get that story and stay out of the way. Politicians are hard to interview since they have a lot to hide. Their goal is to get through the hour without telling too much." The political process is one of control, and "politicians want to control the picture the public has of them."

"The prince of access," Brian asserts the public's right to see public officials and those who attempt to influence public policy in action. Agreeing with Woodrow Wilson's goal of "open covenants openly arrived at," Brian extends that principle beyond international relations to all levels of government. Renowned for his mild-as-milk demeanor on camera, he becomes exercised when he talks about those who resist coverage, in government or outside.[13] Brian was successful in embarrassing the journalists from the Radio-TV Correspondents Association, who usually argue for openness to allow C-SPAN cameras to cover the group's annual dinner. With that scalp on his belt, he went after the more exclusive Gridiron Club. So far, the best he has been able to do is set up a stakeout and catch people as they arrived. Brian has little legal basis for demanding access, so he uses humor and public ridicule as his tools. In 2003, while receiving the Freedom of Speech Award from the Media Institute, he proposed the tongue in cheek "Lens-cap Award," for those entities most vigorous in keeping the cameras away. He singled out for derision the Gridiron Club, the U.S Supreme Court (with a "special mention" for Justice Antonin Scalia, his old friend who nonetheless routinely bars cameras from his speeches), the Senate Appropriations Committee (for barring cameras from its markup sessions where the final form is legislation is crafted), and the Democratic and Republican Campaigns committees (for their skittishness in allowing cameras at their fund-raising events).[14]

Brian takes pride in his ability to fire off questions, shut up, and listen. He sets a standard for the interviewers of his staff that leaves them breathless. His record is fifty-seven questions in a one-hour program.

Rapid-fire questioning carries over to his personal life. Brian's nieces and nephews have become accustomed to, if not comfortable with, his questioning on public affairs. One niece remembers sitting around Brian's mother's house as she lay dying of cancer. The temperature was very high. But it was the "machine-gun pressure from Uncle Brian that created beads of sweat on our foreheads."

Perhaps Brian's greatest achievement with the board of directors lay in getting them to agree to no board involvement in C-SPAN's journalistic decisions as to what should go on the air. Brian realized that if C-SPAN were seen as the political vehicle of the cable industry or the government's mouthpiece, its credibility would be nil.

WHAT MAKES IT NEWSWORTHY?

C-SPAN is a "no-personality zone" when it comes to its on air staff, guests, and choice of stories to pursue. Brian is proud of the fact that while the commercial networks overindulged on the O. J. Simpson trial, he remained a nonentity on C-SPAN. While Anna Nicole Smith's life and death clogged the commercial airwaves, C-SPAN stood moot and seemingly unaware of the popular culture bombshell. Paris Hilton's misdeeds would have gone unmentioned on C-SPAN if it were not for the intersection of irresponsible behavior and questions about the fairness of the legal system. Once people began questioning whether Hilton was treated less harshly because of her celebrity status, it raised the kind of public affairs questions Brian finds relevant.

WORTH NOTING

Brian's rationale for beginning *Booknotes*, in 1989, sounds like much of his talk about the founding of C-SPAN. Others were not doing a good job getting beyond sound bites when discussing books on television. Viewers needed more information to make better decisions, in this case, in selecting books to read. "There are a lot of authors interviewed elsewhere on TV," he told Frazier Moore of the Associated Press, "but after the typical six-minute interviews, you'll never know if the book is any good or not. You won't even know if the author can write. You won't even necessarily know if the author can speak. After watching an interview like that, I find I'm left wanting more."[15] More information is a passion for a man who admits how little he actually learned in college. He just wasn't ready then.

The creation of *Booknotes* required a change in Brian's outlook before a change in corporate philosophy. In 1986, recently retired Supreme Court Justice Warren Burger took over the U.S. Constitution bicentennial celebration. In an attempt to get the word out, Burger created an advisory committee of media executives and Brian was asked to join. Admitting little interest in the celebration, Brian agreed since it would be a good "opportunity to observe the well-known chief justice up close."[16] Little did he realize how much the experience would change him and the organization he founded. He remembers being a struggling 'C' student, intimidated by incredibly bright students in college. "I read all the classics [but] I just wasn't ready. I had no idea what I was doing."[17] One day, Burger handed each member of the committee a copy of Catherine Drinker Bowen's classic,

Miracle at Philadelphia. At forty-five years of age and a busy executive, Brian admitted that "Books were a luxury for which I, like many people, had little time . . . the book lit a fire under me. Midway through, I was hooked enough to want to know more."[18] It humanized the constitution and drew him in.

There are few times when one looks back at one book as the inspiration for a change in lifestyle. Brian associates his love of reading and the eventual development of a book component on C-SPAN to Tom Wolff's *Bonfire of the Vanities.* Once into it, finishing the book became an overwhelming passion, leading him to get up in the middle of the night to read. He ended up in a race with one of his board members to see who could read it faster. Brian still praises Wolff as "a prophet whose predictions have all become true." The fire pushing him from an infrequent reader of popular books to a passionate reader of serious tomes became ferocious and Brian went from a casual reader to a man with a mission. Just as the religious convert is the most fervent proselytizer, he sought out numerous ways to get his staff and viewers to read.

Brian was nothing if not prepared when he walked into a *Booknotes* interview. While many interviewers have done little more than skim an author's book or rely on a quick briefing by a staff member, Brian prepared for *Booknotes* by carefully reading often ponderous tomes at a pace of at least one a week for sixteen years. His efforts add up to a small library of over 800 serious books. His marginal notes were extensive and generated insightful questions which would have been considered minutiae in most other settings. When confronted with the fact that Larry King intentionally refuses to read a guest's book, Brian explains without criticizing, "I don't read them to impress other people. I read them because I want to learn something. If I read a book, it's a much different interview than if I don't. You can do it the other way successfully. But if you read the book, there's all kinds of stuff hidden in those books that most people don't see. It often generates some of the best interviews."[19]

With a tone more of description than disappointment, Brian points out that he "committed about 1.8 years of my life to reading books for the series."[20] Brian's "catches" on *Booknotes* represent an impressive list of authors and public leaders including Margaret Thatcher, Mikkhail Gorbachev, Richard Nixon, George H. W. Bush, Jimmy Carter, and Bill Clinton. While each aimed at hawking a book, authors found themselves in a different environment than the typical book tour interview. Rather than sound bites and pleasantries, Brian had the luxury of follow-up questions and introspection. The focus on the author was clear and intentional. In the typical *Booknotes* program, Brian appeared on the air for about four minutes and his guest for fifty-six minutes.[21] Brian has learned that for C-SPAN viewers, his interviews are not about him. Both his preparation and conduct of the interview reveal Brian in the pure learning mode. He wants to know both the obvious and the context. With both a twinkle of humor and a dash of pride, staff members saw *Booknotes* as part of "C-SPAN University." One media observer commented that watching Brian "conduct an hour-long interview reminds me of seeing people put together a jigsaw puzzle, systematically and with a sense of purpose, as they make sure that one piece will lead logically to the next one."[22] Being invited to appear on *Booknotes* clearly sold books, but it was a one-shot opportunity. Brian's self-created rules specified that the books must be nonfiction, public affairs-oriented, hardback, and that an author could only appear once in his or her life.

Authors' desires to land a spot on *Booknotes* were only surpassed by the holy grail of appearing on Oprah to schlock their book. As Brian remembers, "When I was doing *Booknotes*, I couldn't go anywhere without an author handing me their book. I'd be in an airport or store and authors would thrust their books on diet or anthropology or self-help in my hands. It wouldn't work anyway, but they hadn't even bothered to see what kinds of books we did."[23]

Brian's interest in the books he reads is real, not a face he puts on to do a job. For many interviewers, a brief author interview ends with the author disgorging a rehearsed "mind dump," as the pressure of the next interview assignment captures his or her attention. Brian's engagement with the subjects of the books he chooses is real and abiding. He explains that "I'll read the book and then sit down with an author and I'll say, 'I've got to do that.' I've got to go find places that he talked about or she talked about in the book . . . I'm a historical tourist now."[24]

While not disparaging formal education, Brian recognizes the potential to learn on one's own. He proudly shows off his *Booknotes*-driven, book-lined office and with a sweep of his hand explains, "There is a whole Ph.D. in this room. *Booknotes* helped fill a big vacuum in my head." Currently the books are organized chronologically in the order of the appearance of their authors on *Booknotes*. For many years, Brian's filing system involved a series of precarious piles. On returning from a trip, Brian found that his staff had ordered bookshelves and turned his office into a mini-library housing books Brian was intimately acquainted with.

Brian recognized the there were two stories he could help tell about every book and that he had a responsibility not to waste his viewer's time. He could focus on the book, both its content and how it was written, or he could focus on the author, how the author got to the place where a book flowed from his or her mind onto paper.

STRAIGHT SHOTS, NO SPEED BUMPS

Interviewing is much like a scientific experiment based on the stimulus-response model. Chemists stimulate compounds by heating them and then measure the response. Physicists stimulate projectiles by subjecting them to a measured thrust and assess the response in terms of speed and distance covered. Interviewers stimulate subjects and then sit back to wait for their response. Although interview subjects with the capacity for reason and creativity are less predictable than inert compounds, interviewers develop a toolkit of stimuli that they believe will result in the kinds of responses that fit their definition of being interesting and newsworthy. The potential stimuli for interviews include the setting, the warm-up, tongue-loosening evidence, the questions, the follow-up, and the interviewer's response.

The setting can be very important. Ambushing an interview subject on the street and demanding answers when he or she does not expect it is likely to get very different responses than carrying out a long-scheduled interview in a comfortable studio. Sitting in an interview subject's office, with all of its memory triggering keepsakes, may lead to responses less likely to happen in some sterile atmosphere. Warming up the interview subject by building rapport has the potential for humanizing the experience and encouraging subjects, especially those who are less experienced, to reveal things they might not otherwise say. Some interviewers believe in confronting interview subjects with documents, pictures, or video clips and asking them to justify and explain the hard "facts." This might involve the revelation of a secret document the interview subject had no idea the interviewer possessed or a quote or clip from the past that seems to be at odds with current views. Presidential candidate John Kerry gave interviewers fodder in 2004 over the seeming inconsistency of implying that voting against wartime funding bills was equivalent to abandoning the troops and then voting against the funding himself. After receiving questions about his vote, he justified his action by saying, "I actually did vote for the $87 billion before I voted against it."[25] Watching politicians squirm has become a national parlor game facilitated by some interviewers.

Brian's "secret" document was the author's own book, filled with notations and obviously carefully read. As one interview subject put it, "During my answers, I kept watching Brian flip through my book looking for another detailed question. I tried to estimate where he was in the book and what the subject might be. I know I could look pretty foolish not being able to illuminate something I had written myself. It must be like defending one's dissertation for a Ph.D., with one competent grand inquisitor."

The questions remain at the heart of every interview. Open-ended questions ("How would you evaluate the president's performance?") give the interview subject a great deal of leeway. This can provide insights one might not expect, but allows avoiding the question by giving a prerehearsed or innocuous answer. Closed-ended questions ("What grade would you give the president: 'A,' 'B,' 'C,' 'D,' or 'F'?") keeps the interview subject on track and forces a clear choice, but reveals none of the nuances of the answer or the rationale behind it. Some interviewers use the opportunity to show off their knowledge and connections more than tapping the experience and expertise of the interview subject. Few answers tell the whole story. Follow-up questions flesh out previous answers. Some interviewers use innocuous follow-ups, such as "Why do you say that?" "Can you explain that a little more?" Others are much more aggressive, looking for inconsistencies or potential areas of conflict. As social interactions, interviews often tempt interview subjects to look to interviewers for signals and validation. Body language and facial expressions indicate to an interview subject whether they are on track. A fidgeting interviewer, no longer taking notes, implies the need for a new direction. An interviewer more interested in his or her prepared notes implies that he or she is not really listening and the follow-ups will not relate to the answers given. Facial expressions send even clearer signals, both on how the interview is going and the interviewer's approval. Some interviewers are well known for "eyebrow editorializing," in which a squint or one raised eyebrow says, "You have got to be kidding."

The three basic approaches to interviewing use different stimuli in different ways. The "gotcha" school of interviewing assumes that interview subjects have something to hide and that the truth has to be pried out of them. Interviewers such as Mike Wallace of CBS's *60 Minutes* uses hidden cameras, ambush interviews on the street, confrontation with documents, tough questions, relentless follow-ups, and clear signals when the interviewer does not view the responses as credible. ABC newsman Sam Donaldson, one of the most aggressive investigative television journalists, justified his approach by commenting: "If you send me to cover a pie-baking contest on Mother's Day, I'm going to ask dear old Mom why she used artificial sweetener in violation of the rules, and while she's at it, could I see the receipt for the apples to prove that she didn't steal them. I maintain that if Mom has nothing to hide, no harm will have been done. But the questions should be asked. Too often, Mom, and presidents—behind those sweet faces—turn out to have stuffed a few rotten apples into the public barrel."[26]

On the other end of the scale is Larry King and his "softball" approach to interviewing. King's CNN show is the program of choice for stars and politicians. They know he will treat them as old friends, direct the questions to the topics they are most interested in answering, ask relatively innocuous questions, and not embarrass the interview subjects with pesky follow-ups or implied interviewer disillusionment. King explains that, "I never attack. Attacking is a gimmick that wears thin. If you probe guests without offending them, you're more likely to get truthful answers to your questions. When you attack, you create hostility and a return thrust, but you don't get much information."[27] Being on Larry King is like going to an old friend's home who wants to maintain the relationship to ensure another visit. King prides himself on exclusive interviews, especially on breaking stories and reticent guests. As King describes it, "I try to ask questions that the guy on the street would want to know, human questions, not 'press conference' questions. My approach is always nonthreatening and nonjudgmental."[28] King is obviously successful in terms of ratings and longevity. It is perhaps unfair to criticize him for not being a journalist, when that is not his goal. The title of his book *How to Talk to Anyone, Anytime, Anywhere* captures his emphasis on conversation, a skill that is different from interviewing. Brian's interviewing approach stands between the "gotcha" and the softball. Although the middle of the road might inherently sound like a good place to be, as the old joke goes, "the only thing in the middle of the road is a yellow line and a lot of dead possum." Brian does not get off the hook for criticism. Those who appreciate the "gotcha" approach feel that he and his staff are not tough enough on guests, while other viewers complain that he is too tough, at least on guests whose political views they agree with. Some argue that some of his questions are so basic as to be insulting. After asking a professor at MIT, "What is MIT?" one reviewer complained that "Lamb sometimes underestimates his audience's knowledge."[29]

The interviewing style for which Brian is now famous emerged out of years of trial and error. He admits that "It's absolutely me. . . . I copied everybody in my early years. I wanted to sound like David Brinkley or Chet Huntley. There came a time . . . when I was in my late teens [when someone told me], 'Will you stop being everybody else and be yourself. You either have a style or you don't. You either have a voice for this business or you don't. Stop trying to be like anybody else.' And I did."[30]

Brian is a seeker of truth and privately expresses frustration with guests who don't answer the question. After years in Washington, he admits that "the thing that gets under my skin more than anything else is that politicians have learned to never answer a question. They've learned to hide. They've figured out that if they wait long enough, they can come back in a month or so and no media will ask them about the earlier controversy."[31]

For better or worse, Brian has created an interview style for himself and expects other hosts to follow his lead.

GUIDANCE FOR HOSTS (AN ABBREVIATED SET OF HIGHLIGHTS FROM C-SPAN TRAINING MATERIAL)

- The majority of the questions should be open-ended.
- Watch the "inside the Beltway" jargon.
- Watch out for "loading" and leading questions.
- Provide a source for statements when possible.
- Don't indicate approval or disapproval of guests' answers.

Brian's interviewing style has been compared to 1950s television detective Jack Webb as having a "just the facts" approach.[32] "He practices an austere brand of reporting and interviewing. He doesn't chat. He doesn't philosophize."[33] In a world of interviewers raised on "gotcha journalism," Brian has little interest in ambushing guests and trying to embarrass them through clever questions. He starts from the premise that open-ended questions about a guest's views, opinions, and goals will generate a great deal more information than trying to box them in with a set of closed-ended yes-and-no questions. He also believes in giving them enough time to answer. While some have expressed the fear that such flexibility makes it possible that C-SPAN will be "used" by guests for their own political purposes, Brian says his goal is to "make it possible for everyone to use us, but in the process they expose their strengths and weaknesses to the public." Brian subscribes to the "marketplace of ideas" concept attributed to Justice Oliver Wendell Holmes Jr. Although Holmes never used the phrase, he promoted the concept of free speech, arguing, "We should be eternally vigilant against attempts to check the expression of opinions that we loathe."[34] In addition, both Holmes and Brian imply that when the full array of ideas appear on the public table, better policy results as the wise and well thought out overwhelm the ignorant and shallow.

Brian is the kind of student all teachers wish for. Although no stellar student while in school, he makes teaching worthwhile by remembering the efforts of those who had him in the classroom. Brian keeps in touch with his old high school teachers and credits them with his basic journalistic skills. Special credit goes to Bill Fraser, his high school journalism teacher. Fraser defined good technique as, "You ask a question and then you listen to that answer, and you act on the answer during the interview before you jump ahead."[35] Fraser expanded his suggestions by encouraging his students to never ask a question with a simple "yes" or "no" answer, ask follow-up questions, give interview subjects enough time to make their point (or perhaps hang themselves), and don't interject your own viewpoint. Brian says Fraser taught him, among other things, that "it's not necessary to ask the questions that will shake the universe. Just ask: Where are you from? How old are you? What did you talk about at the dinner table? What were your parents like?"[36]

While the Federal Communications Commission or Parent's Television Council count the number of four-letter words on the air, the height of indecency on C-SPAN results from asking a closed-ended question. They are counted and reported as a not too gentle encouragement to "go and sin no more." Brian firmly believes that if you ask a closed-ended, yes-and-no question, "they'll give you a yes-or-no answer. . . . Our philosophy is to ask the question, listen to the answer, and try to follow-up on the answer instead of your next question . . . [otherwise], you'll miss tremendous opportunities."

Brian's commitment to context is both a luxury of long interviews and recognition that a guest is not just a name with a current affiliation, but "a much wider package" of experiences and connections. He recognizes that who you are depends to a large degree on where you are from and where you hope to be going. The initial foray into broader understanding of guests involves asking where they were born, where they went to school, and where they have worked. Finding out about his or her relevant family ties enriches the tapestry of the guest's life. Rather than simply introducing journalist and professor Steve Roberts on the basis of his profession, Brian explains that he would ask questions to draw out the fact that Roberts is married to fellow journalist Cokie Roberts, whose mother and father were members of Congress (Hale and Lindy Boggs) and whose brother (Tommy Boggs) is a successful Washington lobbyist.

Interview questions set a tone. When Brian "asks questions about an author's family, which have become a staple in the Brian interview, the writers invariably drop whatever scripted comments they have—many acknowledge cramming before a Brian interview. Their voices change. They become people instead of experts on some esoteric topic."[37]

Part of Brian's appeal is his interest in others. When he is talking to someone, they are his main focus. He is not always looking around the room for a new entrant in hopes of "trading up." He realizes that the sweetest music to anyone's ears is their own name and the most interesting story is about them. Known for his skill at remembering names, Brian plays it as less of a parlor trick than a reflection of how he deals with people. When one of his old friends asked him for his trick and suggested word association or mnemonics, Brian cut him short, saying factually, not judgmentally, "All those gimmicks can help, but they will never work for you because you don't care."

A key to Brian's interviewing is to listen. We have all heard the interviewer more interested in framing the next question than in listening to the answer to the last one. For example, the interviewer, after receiving the answer "dead" to the question "How are your parents?" fills the gap with an inappropriate "great," and then goes on to another question, whose answer he or she is not really interested in either. Not listening is more than rudeness to Brian, it undermines the ability to ask relevant follow-up questions to fill in gaps. Brian's style emerged out of the school of hard knocks. Bad experiences serve as good platforms for learning. One time when interviewing the water commissioner in Mission Viejo, California, Brian tried to enliven a pretty deadly session by looking over his shoulder and asking, "How many gallons of water in the reservoir" behind them held. The commissioner admitted he had no idea. With the throwaway question buying him little thinking time, Brian went on to a few more questions without hitting pay dirt. Forgetting his initial foray and its answer, Brian asked again about the capacity of the reservoir. The perturbed commissioner blurted out, "You asked me that a few minutes ago. I didn't know then and I don't know now." Neither Brian, the commissioner, nor the audience found the interview very pleasing. For the Brian, the lesson rang clear. If you are going to ask a question, listen to the answer.

In an era where journalists often have their own agendas and skip through interviews almost oblivious to what was said, Brian's willingness to listen sets him apart. As one fellow journalist said, "In a roomful of journalists, it is easy to spot Brian Lamb. He's the one who is listening."[38] The Midwestern nostrum that God gave you two ears and one mouth, so act accordingly, finds practical application in his approach. Interview subjects are often taken aback that "he really listened to me." After weeks on book tours, armed with a set of talking points, they fight to get into each brief interview; actually being engaged in a conversation is a new experience.

Brian has been called "America's best listener."[39] Good listening takes effort and great patience. In an era of sound bites, rapid cutaways, and hyperstimulation of the audience, silence is an anathema. The normal rules don't apply to Brian Lamb and, even more of a rare occurrence, he accepts conversational rules set by others. In recalling his unbroken string of having interviewed every president since Lyndon Johnson, he has special respect for Bill Clinton as an interview subject. He recalls that Clinton "would sometimes ponder for 30 seconds before answering a question." Rather than being upset, Brian reflects, "I thought that was terrific, not to have to answer immediately."[40]

Brian's interviews with presidents don't fit the typical pattern. He tries to avoid contact with the public relations "handlers" bent on suggesting questions and trying to negotiate out of bounds topics. He would rather come in with no fanfare, sit down, and carry out the interview.

Brian believes in doing his homework, whether it is reading an entire book for *Booknotes*, reviewing dozens of morning papers, or talking to people on the street.

He practices a "university of the real world" style of information gathering. In assessing the level of public knowledge, he is not drawn to national surveys with their scientific analysis. Following footnotes, paging through dusty tomes or Google searches leave him cold. Brian would rather go into the field and experience the public's perspectives firsthand. On a trip to California, he realized his own lack of knowledge about its total population. He began asking everyone in sight, "What is the population of California." The answers ranged from one million to three billion. It took quite awhile to find someone with an accurate estimate of 35 million.

Schmoozing, building rapport, and loosening up guests is a way of life in the media. Some interviewers give guests a heads-up as to the questions they will be asked, while others even encourage interview subjects to suggest questions. In a classic case of developing a "just between us" confidential talk between friends, journalist Connie Chung made big headlines by chatting with then-House Speaker Newt Gingrich's mother for over two hours and then getting her to say that Gingrich thought Hillary Clinton was a "bitch."[41] In stark contrast, Brian deliberately refuses to talk to his interview subjects before the program. The guests move from a minimal "green room," where they have been waiting, to an equally minimal set.[42]

Brian has become the practitioner of a unique interviewing style that he imposes by example and exhortation on C-SPAN hosts. He strongly feels that many star interviewers "get in the way of the interview subject," as the interviewers use their few minutes to score points by asking "gotcha questions" that will pry out a newsworthy sound-bite tidbit designed to embarrass or challenge. First, Brian begins each interview with a sincere desire to know about the interview subject. Second, he uses very basic questions emanating from Journalism 101, "Who" (are you?), "What" (did you do?), "When" (was that?), and "Why" (did you do it?). He mixes up the order and uses different wording, but the basics are always there. His questions are always open-ended, allowing the interview subject to frame the answer and explore its nuances.

His interest and style are clear when asked to describe his technique to students. He pulls a student out of the crowd and asks, "Who are you?" "Why did you decide to go to xxx University?" "What are you majoring in?" "Why?" As the student begins to open up, you can see Brian almost forgetting about the fact that he is demonstrating a technique as he and often the other students are drawn into this student's life story. The roommate of one of the students chosen to be Brian's subject commented in amazement, "I have lived with him for two years and I did not know most of those things." Another student commented, "After being peppered with questions by Mr. Lamb, I felt like a deflated balloon with all the air sucked out of me." Early television personality Art Linkletter made a career proving that, with a microphone before them, "kids say the darndest things." Brian has expanded that generalization to adults, many of whom are sophisticated media manipulators caught off guard when they are allowed plenty of time to disclose their thoughts.

There are a lot of people who it would be fascinating to see Brian interview. It has almost become a parlor game speculating on the kinds of questions he would ask of well-known figures that would never be part of interview protocol on any other network. As David Brooks speculated, "You get the impression that if Brian interviewed Jesus, the first questions out of his mouth would be: 'It's said you fed the multitudes with loaves and fishes. What kind of fish was that? How many people does it take to make up a multitude?'"[43] Brian serves as the epitome of Mark Twain's advice that "He who asks a question is a fool for a moment. He who never asks a question is a fool forever." He is not afraid to show his ignorance or to serve as a surrogate "fool" by asking basic questions. A caller suggested that he title his autobiography, "Who Was Abraham Lincoln?"[44] after Brian asked that question of a guest. Even that inquiry seems less silly when one considers the different depths of personality and meaning it could unleash.

Brian views a good interview as one that will inform the average viewer. Brian has a clear idea of his audience. In earlier years, he claimed to be asking questions for his mother, an intelligent, but not well-educated person. Brian's lack of ego shows up vividly in his interview style. He faced a particular challenge when he created *Booknotes*. He quickly argues, "This is not a show done for intellectuals. A lot of people thought it was in the beginning. People say to me, 'These are the same questions I want to ask.' It's because they're so basic. . . . I don't care whether people think I'm bright or not."[45]

Brian really tries to find the questions middle-Americans want answered. As a "Rolodex rodeo rider," Brian keeps in touch with dozens of friends on a regular basis. Before interviewing Bill Clinton, he canvassed a number of his Indiana friends asking, "What would you ask Bill Clinton?" When one responded, "Mr. President, if you were interviewing Abraham Lincoln, what would you ask him?" Brian asked the question, which became "the" question reported in the news. True to his style, Brian went one step further, crediting his friend.

"If there is an unspoken theme of C-SPAN's coverage it is reveal, reveal, reveal. Brian always asks who owns what. He asks who is married to whom. He rarely fails to mention where someone used to work and who his or her parents are, if that is relevant."[46]

C-SPAN tends to break all the rules of television. Who else would have had stutterer P. F. Bentley, author of a photo book on President Clinton, on the air. He would not have passed the screening call from the associate producer for most programs. As Brian recalls it, it was "one solid hour of stuttering, [and] we even talked about his stuttering on the show."[47]

Stories about Brian's interviews are legion. When interviewing an Iranian journalist by phone during the height of the Iraq War, Brian took the journalist, who had been describing the desperation of the Iraqis, by surprise when he asked him if knew what the unemployment in Iraq was.[48] He threw a curve at Jimmy Carter, asking him to analyze his role as a father.

Brian's bland on-air personality seems to equip him to be an unflappable interviewer. Although the *Booknotes* interviews were not broadcast live, they were not edited. Different interviews stand out for different reasons. One of the strangest in Brian's memory was Clifford Stoll, author of *Silicon Snake Oil: Second Thoughts on the Information Highway*. Brian noticed that Stoll's hands were filled with numbers and notes. Curious, Brian asked a question about this, and it propelled Stoll to stand up and hide behind his chair. What does one do on an interview show when the interview subject is AWOL? With no panic, Brian simply waited him out, and the interview eventually resumed.[49] *Booknotes* has placed Brian in the role of "America's Literary Grand Inquisitor."[50]

SO WHAT DO YOU THINK ABOUT THE WEATHER?
BRIAN LAMB INTERVIEWS THE PRESIDENT

Lamb's interview questions are unlike almost any other interviewer. They force the interview subject to think about nuances and implications often missing in the rushed format of sound-bite journalism.

Among his questions of recent presidents are the following.

- William Jefferson Clinton, February 17, 1995 (available at http://www.presidency.ucsb.edu/ws/?pid=51000)

  > Lamb: Mr. President, we're talking in and around President's Day, so I want to see if you could tell us the purpose of having this little thing on your desk that involves another president—"Dewey Defeats Truman."
  >
  > Lamb: What's the first thing you'd ask Jack Kennedy if you could talk to him today?
  >
  > Lamb: Based on what you've learned after being here two years and—assume you run again next time around, would you do something different? There was a lot written, for instance, when you went on MTV and somebody asked you what kind of underwear you wore, and then for weeks afterwards, it was written about all the time. Are there things like that you're to avoid, or did that bother you?

- George W. Bush January 27, 2005 (available at: http://www.q-and-a.org)

  > Lamb: What role have books played in your presidency?
  >
  > Lamb: How much reading do you do a day, and what time of day do you read?
  >
  > Lamb: Your dad—do you talk much about the presidency with him?
  >
  > Lamb: Can I ask you about indecency? You've got an opportunity to appoint a new chairman of the Federal Communications Commission. Michael Powell is leaving, and you might have other appointments; you have five commissioners. And one of the big issues moving around Capitol Hill is indecency. And I want to ask you, how far do you think government should go in telling people who use the airwaves, the broadcast stations, what can be said?

Lamb: Last question. A lot of people said, if you really want to understand Ronald Reagan, you have to go to the ranch. He spent 345 days in eight years there. You spent, according to Mark Knoller of CBS, who keeps tabs of this, something like 297 days at your ranch. . . . Do we have to go to the ranch to find out who George W. Bush is?

COUNTERING TERRORISM

One's reaction to criticism tells a great deal about them. While Brian's mother undoubtedly purveyed the good Midwestern advice of "sticks and stones may break my bones, but names will never hurt me," or "don't dignify the attack with a response," Brian's ego is so deeply entwined with C-SPAN charges, especially those he feels unfair, that they don't simply roll off his back. In June 2007, conservative talk show host Mike Savage (pseudonym of Michael Alan Weiner), founder of radio's *The Savage Nation*, took on Brian in public. Savage's vitriol began when C-SPAN did not cover his prerecorded speech when receiving *Talkers Magazine* Freedom of Speech Award, an award Brian received in 2000. With no input from Brian, but based on long-term policy, C-SPAN's programming staff cut away because Savage did not show up to give the speech live, instead sending in an eleven-minute DVD, which he soon began selling on his website. C-SPAN offered to cover a live presentation of the speech, but Savage screamed censorship and began marshalling for an all-out attack on C-SPAN and Brian. By implication, C-SPAN became part of the "progressive movement," which he likens to Nazi Storm troopers, "the same rabble that brought Hitler to power."[51] As C-SPAN's telephone lines began to light up and e-mails became clogged, Brian mounted a counterattack, using his favorite tool—information. He simply turned the incoming e-mails back on the senders. Without censorship and expanding the vocabulary usually heard on C-SPAN, he began reading e-mails such as the following on the air:

You are a "dickhead."
You are an "ass loser communist."
You are a Nazi and a Stalinist and probably a homosexual.
As a taxpayer, I demand that you air the freedom speech by Dr. Savage.
I pay your salary and you have no right censoring programs based on your political beliefs.

Brian let the ad hominem attacks roll off his back and only confronted the misinformation, pointing out that C-SPAN is privately funded.[52]

While Brian respects his audience, he recognizes their personal short-comings and foibles. He observes that "people who are angry with the host are often angry because they worry about the dumb guy down the street. . . . They have figured out what's right and wrong, and . . . they want me to correct it for the guy down the street 'cause they don't think he's smart or with it." He offers the same charitable view of guests. A pretty good judge of human character, Brian's even-handed treatment of guests is more than manners or Midwestern "nice." He admits, "The more angry you get with a guest, the more sympathetic the audience gets toward the guest, and the more angry they get toward the host."[53]

THE VIEW FROM THE OTHER END OF THE MIKE

The consummate interviewer, Brian shows great charity toward others who have interviewed him. He remembers rare instances of being misquoted and chalks up most differences to "honest misunderstanding or differences in interpretation." His greatest frustration lies with the tendency to give him too much credit. Aside from his staff, he would like to give credit to the many board members who have backed him up. Unfortunately he finds that "interviewer's eyes glaze over" when he starts to outline the unique contri-butions of such individuals. "They are just not interested and it is their loss."

A BREAK IN THE FACADE

The passive face of Brian Lamb can be ruffled. During a program with a group of students, Brian opened the phone lines and on came the disem-bodied voice of President Reagan saying, "I just came upstairs to the study and turned on the set, and there you were, and I watched long enough to hear several questions that shows your concern about the exclusionary rule." Having the "audience-member-in-chief" as a viewer was a great shot in the arm to the fledgling C-SPAN and to Brian himself. Reviewing the tape twenty years later, Brian chuckled, "I had an expression on my face when that call came in that I've never seen anywhere. . . . I remember it like it was yesterday."[54]

Brian's interview with Richard Nixon in 1992 on his book *Seize the Moment: America's Challenge in a One-Superpower World* stood out as a highlight for both Brian and his staff. Despite having worked in the Nixon White House, Brian had never met Nixon before interviewing him on the air. The interview was done in two one-hour shoots, sandwiched between a nap and a lunch for Nixon. Some of the staff refused to leave the office for fear they would miss seeing the controversial former president. After the interview, the younger staff stood in line to have their copies of his book autographed, while the older staff held back.

USING THE BRIDGE

Brian does not bristle at the assertion that political interests "use" C-SPAN for their own purposes. He simply argues, "We are open to anyone using us. It is up to the public to judge whether they are right or wrong." During the 2000 campaign, those opposing Al Gore jumped on an interview with Brian where Gore wrongly identified his sister as the first Peace Corps volunteer. Brian asked Gore to repeat the assertion, and he did. The story ended up with limited "legs," showing up primarily on conservative websites as one more piece of evidence of Gore's purported inability to tell the truth.[55] In Brian's view, "We are not interested in embarrassing them [the lawmakers] or protecting. We show exactly what is going on without trying to create a drama or an image of what doesn't exist."[56]

Frank Greer, Bill Clinton's campaign director, was so impressed with Clinton's performances on C-SPAN that he adopted the C-SPAN approach during the New Hampshire primary. Greer says, "We bought thirty minutes of time—on commercial stations . . . it was unscreened phone calls, just like C-SPAN. . . . As the campaign progressed, you saw the networks—especially the morning shows—following the format of C-SPAN. . . . I really look to Brian Lamb as a visionary in the world of media. . . . I think he transformed the whole character of the campaign."[57]

Brian has a soft spot for the written word, giving journalists and book authors numerous opportunities to express their views on the network. When it comes to actual political events, he has maintained, in political scientist Larry Sabato's words, "a pundit free zone [where one goes] to get to watch the event without the incessant, obnoxious chatter of anchors and analysts, sometimes taking over the event as though what they have to say is more important than what's happening."[58]

Once Ross Perot established a base and got a "kick start" on publicity for his 1992 presidential bid, the conventional media picked up his story. Between May and July 1992, his coverage exceeded that of Bill Clinton's candidacy. Part of Perot's later problems with the media stemmed from C-SPAN. After a particularly heated appearance on "Meet the Press," Brian interviewed Perot for one and one-half hours in his Texas offices. Brian attempted to walk the fine line between C-SPAN's objective approach to interviewing and the need to get Perot to answer key charges he had avoided. Without making any new charges, Brian simply asked Perot to respond to a series of charges in the other media. Perot's answers on that program seemed either inconsistent or at odds with other evidence. The C-SPAN interview served as the basis for a spate of negative stories in the commercial media. With the media hitting so close to home, Perot began to think about dropping out. After his departure from the race in July and eventual reentry, coverage dropped.

Brian seeks the holy grail of balance and fairness with vigor and flexibility. If his current approach does not seem to be working, he is willing to shift gears and try another approach. He views C-SPAN as facilitating a national conversation on public affairs, but is not above guiding that conversation to make sure a wide range of views are included. When the call-in programs began to become imbalanced geographically, he set up geographic lines and had the hosts shift back and forth between them. During the 1996 campaign, when conservative callers began to dominate, he set up lines to support President Clinton and former Senator Bob Dole. When callers charged him with a liberal bias, they touched a raw nerve. "Brian, who typically shows as much emotion as a face on Mount Rushmore, appeared almost testy as he explained to caller after caller that C-SPAN's mission is balance and fairness, not advocacy."[59] To another who called charging that "You don't get out of Washington and see how this country is falling apart," Brian struck back, "How do you know I don't get out . . . of this town?"[60]

JUST A PLAIN OLD BRIDGE

Although well prepared and literate, no one would consider Brian a smooth talker. "He speaks with a gravelly Midwestern monotone, which he interrupts a bit too often with an unglamorous 'achemm!' to clear his throat. He has all the charisma of a test pattern, and none of the color."[61] While some may criticize his "performance," they forget that the Midwestern "accent" has carried dozens of national news anchors to stardom and that there is something comforting to have a guest in our living room who talks like a real person.

Brian takes pride in being from Middle America and broadcasting to them. When asked about the choice of American music to be played during roll call votes, he reveals that it is intentional. The audience "doesn't want those dead Germans." He also takes pride in staying in tune with the pulse of the audience and that he deals with them honestly pointing out that "I've never knowingly told them something on the air that wasn't true."

Being on the air serves as a tonic for Brian. In the early years, the frustrations with building a network would get to him and ruffle his stoic facade. His staff remembers him saying, "We are going on the air." Brian would "sit there for three hours and his whole mood would change and he would suddenly be recharged and happy again because he likes talking to people and finding out about them."

Brian does his interviewing in a sparse studio. "The interview room is not unlike a confessional. It's a small space—about 12-feet square—that holds two chairs, a small table, and some cameras manipulated from the control booth. The walls are wrapped in black velvet, and no one else is there except Brian and his guest."[62]

Booknotes eschews the fancy sets with "eye candy" views. The setup provided no distraction and an intimate setting. As soon as a robotic camera became available, even the cameraman was evicted from the studio. Among its rules is the use of one continuous taping with no breaks or retakes. The exceptions prove the rule. An interview with Amity Shales, former *Wall Street Journal* editorial writer, about her book, *The Greedy Hand*, posed a technical problem. A technician pushed the wrong button and ten minutes were lost. She came back for a retape and played the game that she had never heard the questions before and the first ten minutes of interview played out the same as the first time.

Brian has long fought the "I and Me" form of journalism. Rather than reporting the news, many journalists get caught up telling how they got a particular story, thus becoming the story themselves. Dan Rather meets with Afghan rebels or interviews Saddam Hussein and spends much of his scarce airtime telling the audiences about the arduous process of getting the story. Newly minted ABC news anchor Bob Woodruff goes to Iraq for an "up close and personal" story on the war, only to get seriously wounded and becomes the story. While such journalism has its defenders, Brian is not one of them. He seeks to step out of the way, serving as a facilitator rather than a participant.

Deadly as it may seem, C-SPAN has an intoxication all its own. It has created, across the country, hundreds of thousands of C-SPAN junkies— hard-core loyalists who savor a good Congressional floor fight, the way true baseball fans love a pitchers' duel. Like that other Creator, Brian made C-SPAN in his own image—committed to the idea that television news should not be delivered in small, glib nuggets.[63]

8

NO STAR SPAN(G)-LED BANTER

We must watch over our modesty in the presence of those
who cannot understand its grounds.

—Jean Rostand (1894–1977)

As heady as appearance on national television might be, Brian Lamb created C-SPAN as a "no star zone." All hosts do double-duty, with ad-
ministrative tasks carrying as much or more weight than on-air hosting.
Brian cringes when anyone refers to him as a celebrity, pointing out that "A
celebrity has an agent. I don't . . . a celebrity makes speeches for money. I
don't . . . celebrities spend a lot of time sending vanity photos to different
publications or taking out ads in newspapers, with their faces on the front
of books. That's something we don't do."[1] Brian boldly asserts, "I am not
Ted Turner, who first built the network on personality."[2] He seems to take
pride in the fact that even the internally funded C-SPAN polls indicate that
he is only known by about two percent of the audience. In his mind, that
is validation of his goal of trying to "stay out of the way."

UNEASY STARDOM

The scene has become familiar. As Brian makes his way through the airport
terminal or subway station, the middle-aged woman obliquely cuts across
the hallway in such a way that a confrontation or collision is inevitable.
Brian had seen the woman eyeing him as he picked up his ticket, gone
through security, and picked up a coffee. He has seen the scene dozens of
times and knows what is coming. The woman has just discretely pointed

him out to her husband. A muffled conversation ensues sprinkled with phrases like, "It sure looks like him," and "If you are so sure, why don't you just ask him." As the two intersect, the woman blurts out, "Aren't you John McCain? You are a hero of mine." By then the husband has arrived to hear him say, "No, I'm Brian Lamb from C-SPAN." With a big smile the older man says, "Yea, I knew it. You're on Headline News, watch it all the time." Patiently Lamb responds, "No that's CNN, I am from C-SPAN, we cover Congress and public affairs." To which the older man responds, "Sure, we watch it all the time, great show." The variations are slight. For a number of years, the misidentification targeted former astronaut and Senator John Glenn, J. Edgar Hoover, or comedian Bob Newhart. At times it is an older couple, one of whom is dispatched to confirm the identification after hushed discussions punctuated by "You do it, no, you do it." Brian is invariably cordial, at times playing along with the misidentification or gently letting them down. He admits that after someone has misidentified him and told him how much that person has done for the country, that "they are so excited that . . . I don't tell them. I am afraid they are going to break down and cry."[3]

The demographics of those who recognize or misrecognize Brian on the street tends toward middle-aged or older. It is no great surprise that he serves as the "blue hairs' heart throb," given data on interest in politics and television viewing. C-SPAN is battling a proliferation of television networks for a declining audience base, especially among younger citizens.

When the media insists on focusing on him, Brian establishes some clear ground rules. He refuses to sit for posed photographs since *Time* printed a "power shot" of him from a low angle with the Capitol gleaming in the background.[4] As a somewhat incongruous testimony to his antipersonality approach, a Washington courier in his bicycle helmet and spandex pants immediately recognized him in an elevator saying, "Mr. Lamb, I want to thank you for keeping your low profile."[5]

While pleased at the recognition on the street, Brian is committed to a channel that does not depend on personalities. He purposely cut back his air time to reduce the personality factor. He prefers not to give interviews, except when it directly relates to C-SPAN. He recognizes that "in order to make news you have to say something unusual—something you wouldn't ordinarily say. You have to give up something to do that and I am not willing to do that."[6] Around the office, he is personable without being a personality. He does not travel with a bevy of aides and regularly makes the rounds of his staff to ask questions, share something he has read, and/or give encouragement. His visits are seen as friendly familiarity as opposed to meddlesome micromanagement.

In a town where thirsting after power and lusting after fame dominates most human interactions, Brian seems truly to be a little uncomfortable with praise or attention. One of his first program innovations was to bring the National Press Club luncheon speeches to the American public. It was pure Lamb, opening the doors to an insider's gathering. Brian had no compunction about expecting speakers to gauge their comments for a national audience, rather than providing the inside dope to the Washington media corps. When given his chance in 1997, Brian was frank, saying, "We started covering these National Press Club luncheon speeches on January 3, 1980. . . . And I am the 1,200th, let me see, 1,122nd speaker, I think, since that time. I never intended to be us here doing this. I am not so sure I want to be here today. But I'll try to make the best of it."[7]

Brian's modesty remains even more surprising when one considers the passel of honorary degrees and awards in his quiver of accolades. It is one thing to have created an important public utility such as C-SPAN, and another to receive recognition for it. Brian remains one of the small American elite invited to dinner at the White House[8] and having been singled out in a presidential speech.[9] While some CEOs could lap up such honors and need double doors put on their offices so as not to scrape the ears on their swelled heads, Brian seems truly unaffected.

LOCAL BOY MAKES GOOD

C-SPAN's trophy cases overflow with awards, while Brian Lamb simultaneously seems pleased and embarrassed by the attention. He is always quick to point out that his staff and board members deserve much of the credit. After November 2007, Brian's modesty will become harder to maintain as he was honored with the Presidential Medal of Freedom, the nation's highest civilian honor. The medal, that's given to those who have made "an especially meritorious contribution to culture, world peace, or national security and other national interests," is designed as an individual honor. Brian's citation confirmed that he "has elevated America's public debate and helped open up our government to citizens across the nation. His dedication to a transparent political system and the free flow of ideas has enriched and strengthened our democracy."

Caught in the throes of victory, Brian was asked like a winning sports star, "What are you going to do now?" The archetypical response, "I'm going to Disney World," remained totally out of character for Brian. The much more Lamb-like response came out, "Come back to work the next morning." It was also clear that he planned to pass the award around to the "260 colleagues and 20 board members who never get a mention, so this is a shared award."[10]

WHERE THE BRIDGE DOES NOT GO

Brian is both surprised and somewhat appalled that people would have any interest in him as a person. He guards his private life jealously. He shucks it off saying, "I guess I am just pretty boring." Writers seeking hooks to his personal proclivities often latch on to his Catholic religion[11] or his Irish ancestry.[12]

Brian is both a large "C" and a small "c" Catholic, appreciating the universality of the church. Unlike his childhood when one was tied to their parish, his loyalty is in no way tied to any one congregation or parish. He worships at any one of the twenty catholic churches in Northern Virginia, formally joining none. He explains, "Frankly, I just like variety."[13]

While it is often true that "the apple doesn't fall very far from the tree," at least part of that truism does not apply to Brian. Growing up in a family that made its living from "demon rum," Brian's role models were a grandfather who was a bartender and a father who owned a tavern and later became a wholesale beer distributor. One might expect Brian to live a life where alcohol played a prominent part. Although once a social drinker, Brian gave up alcohol completely in his 50s, explaining, "Just looking ahead, I said there is no reason [to drink], I've enough things to look forward to. Might as well not look forward to a disease from smoking and drinking."[14]

Brian's personal life reveals few surprises, exemplifying structure, routine, and precision. There is little "wild and crazy" about the boy from Lafayette. As one staff member put it, "It is hard to imagine Brian with apple juice running down his face, but I had never seen anyone eat an apple or a pear with a knife and fork before."

For all his interest in politics, Brian admits that he would not be the kind of person to call in to C-SPAN. He has no need to hear his own voice. He has only called in to two call-in programs. In one case, it was a music program asking a question about country music to which he knew the answer. The other time occurred in London on a program taking London to task for being dirty. Brian waited twenty-five minutes to defend London and expressed disgust with the filth in New York at that time. That said, Brian asserts "I would not call a call-in show in this country about politics" harboring no desire "to get on the record with what my views are."

Who is the real Brian Lamb? To some degree it depends on whether the cameras are rolling. On air, he exudes bland calmness. His staff point out that "He is a very fun-loving person, but people won't see that side because he chooses not to have that play into his political world." It is not quite Dr. Jekyll and Mr. Hyde, but virtually everyone having close contact with Brian comments on the dramatic difference between his on-air and in-person demeanor. The descriptors of Brian on air fill a small lexicon with terms such as: "serious," "gray," "a test pattern without the color." One of his key staff members remembers trying to loosen up with notes while he was on the air saying, "smile," or "no one wants a scowl at 7:00 AM," only to conclude that the serious demeanor was his "default expression." In person, Brian is personable, humorous, and very caring.

In the early years, Brian was not known for his sense of humor. The onscreen blandness hid a pixie-like penchant for challenging others in private. John Splaine remembers opening Brian's car door for a drive to the National Press Club. "As I leaned over to pick up the Julio Iglesias tape on the seat, Brian barked out 'Give me that tape.' It sounded like he felt I was stealing it." Soon his serious demeanor switched to a big smile as Brian's game of "gotcha" played out. In the same vein, George Buss, Abraham Lincoln impersonator, and Rich Sokup, Stephen Douglas impersonator, were taken aback at the end of a visit to Brian's office with the challenge, "You guys didn't steal anything did you?" For a moment, they thought he was serious before Brian broke up.

In a town where a successful social engagement consists of how many people one can pitch their story to, Brian turns the tables, attempting to gain more information about others than he gives up about himself. A good amateur psychologist, he recognizes that most people are more interested in themselves than in others. He works on the unspoken rule, "I know everything about myself, but I don't know much about them." After a long conversation where the other person has gained little information about him, but has spilled his guts about his hopes, activities, and frustrations, it is not uncommon for the individual to say, "It has really been great talking to you." Brian has no temptation to correct the statements to indicate the person was "talking at" him since he has learned a great deal.

WILL THE REAL BRIAN LAMB PLEASE STAND UP

Those writing about Brian rack their brains for adequate descriptors. Some play in his name, pointing out that he is "more like a Lamb than a Lion," others search the lexicon for other descriptors:

"Laid back demeanor and Midwestern common sense."[1]
"A populist . . . more in the mold of Johnny Carson than of Huey Long."[2]
"A man to reason with, not to bang against."[3]
"One of the last true boy scouts."[4]
"An ascetic."[5]
"The mayor of America's Town Hall."[6]
"The mildest-mannered host."[7]

SOURCES

1. "In Person—The Mayor of America's Town Hall: Brian P. Lamb," *National Journal*, November 23, 1991, p. 2875.
2. Ibid.
3. Colman McCarthy, "Pure C-SPAN," *Washington Post*, November 5, 1994, p. A15.
4. Nancy Traver, "No Glitz, No Glamour," *Time*, August 24, 1992, p. 29.
5. *National Journal*.
6. Ibid.

It is hard to imagine who would play Brian in a movie. Anthony Hopkins has the skill and looks, but would probably damage *his* career playing someone who would not scare or intimidate anyone. His "balding, with deepset eyes, and a tepid gaze,"[15] suggest Bob Newhart, but as soon as Newhart broke into a droll joke, no one would believe his portrayal. Although there is a bit of a resemblance, no one would believe that Steve Martin's "wild and crazy guy" could be morphed into Brian's ascetic approach to work and life. As media critic Howard Kurtz put it, "Brian is a priest of sorts," denying himself some of the so-called pleasures people associate with those having notoriety and the resources to indulge themselves. As one former staff member put it, "He doesn't drink, doesn't smoke, isn't married [at that time], and has no kids. He sets the tone,"[16] and for the entire organization. The image of Brian as the stoic, stone-faced observer applies more to his on-camera persona. "Brian is funnier and more animated in person than he appears on television, where he seems to flatten out his personality. Even off-camera though, one could never imagine Brian as a bearer of whoopee cushions or purveyor of even slightly off-color jokes."

MY BROTHER'S KEEPER

Perhaps no story reveals the differences between Jim and Brian Lamb better than their approach to a jointly owned vacation cabin in Maine. Sensitive to the concerns of his new neighbors about the invasion of outsiders, Brian immediately tried to ingratiate himself with the local residents, attending town meetings, learning his neighbors' names, but never capitalizing on his stardom. During one town meeting when Jim accompanied him, Brian spent most of the time saying, "Jim, don't say anything."

One day, Jim looked out and saw a red surveyor's stake in the middle of their property. Marching out with indignation, he loosened it from the ground and threw it in the woods. When the surveyor returned, Jim proclaimed no knowledge of the offending stake. Brian, the paragon of acting properly, was apoplectic, arguing, "We are the only outsiders in town, we need to get along." A few days later the red stake appeared again and just as quickly disappeared. The next Christmas, Brian opened up his present from Jim to find the missing stake cut up in pieces.

Jim constantly keeps his brother on his toes, reveling in upsetting Brian's sense of propriety and his ability to undermine it. Even after all these years, there is a gullibility on which Jim is a master of capitalizing. When speaking publicly, Brian likes question-and-answer formats, probably out of the humble view that "why should I decide what other people learn about?" When Jim is in the audience, Brian cringes, knowing he will come up with something like, "Why don't you tell the monkey story?" Jim knows that Brian would never tell a raunchy story not fit for mixed company, but likes to see Brian squirm. Jim loves to call Brian, implying he has just revealed something inappropriate. After being interviewed for a story on Brian, Jim called saying, "Gee, Brian, I was not sure what to say. They asked why you were not married, and I said you were a little light in the loafers." Brian shot back aghast, "You didn't Jim; No, you didn't." Jim's big belly laugh eventually let him off the hook.

Jim's boisterous voice, wide circle of friends, and "hale fellow, well met" demeanor hid a darker side. Heavy drinking and drug experimentation caught up with him in 2007. Far from abandoning his brother, Brian served as a loyal supporter and quiet cheerleader, reveling in his "bravery and courage" in going through rehabilitation. Brian revealed no embarrassment as to what the publicity would do to him or the family name, but rather recognized the challenges in his brother's life and the steps he was taking to overcome them.

LOYALTY

Celebrity can disassociate one from old friends and family. Brian endeavors mightily not to let that happen, keeping the lines of communication open with phone calls and visits. His ties to Lafayette and Jefferson High School run deep. He never forgot the debt he felt he owed toward the community, school, and teachers. Whenever asked to come back for a retirement, funeral, wedding, or award ceremony, he tries to be there. Communities like to take pride in "local boy makes good," reveling in someone who *was* from the community. Locals in Lafayette are more likely to say that Brian Lamb *is* from there. At social events, he talks to everyone and makes him or her feel comfortable. He is almost by nature drawn to the outsiders in the crowd. Once he finds them, he asks questions they are comfortable with. As with his interviews, Brian strongly believes that everyone has an interesting story to tell. The key is getting them to tell it. He acts as if everyone, from the busboy to the guest of honor, is equal.

For many Lafayette residents, Brian is not a star. He neither expects to be treated as such nor is C-SPAN part of his old neighbors' regular viewing habits. As he walks almost anonymously around the streets, there is a glint of recognition, but few know whether it is from having seen him on television or passing him regularly on the street.

Brian is proud of his hometown. As part of the opening of the Abraham Lincoln Museum in Springfield, Illinois, he brought the C-SPAN cameras for a live tour. Standing in front of a map outlining the route of Lincoln's funeral train, Brian squealed with glee, "Gee, it went through my hometown of Lafayette, Indiana."

Friendships run deep in Brian's order of priorities. He maintains personal bridges by keeping in touch with old friends regularly by phone. He is seldom too busy and never disinterested in receiving phone calls from dozens of close friends. As a testament to his accessibility, one friend commented, "I often hesitate to call my kids for fear of being too intrusive or interrupting something. I never have the same feeling about Brian. I know he will be glad to hear from me and take time for a call." One friend tells of unexpectedly seeing Brian across the street as they were crossing at a stoplight. Brian grasped his hand in the middle of the street and an animated conversation ensued. It took a cacophony of honking horns to shake Brian from the joy of seeing an old friend and alert him that they were blocking traffic. As one old friend put it, "While some people go off to 'become someone,' and in the process become someone completely different, Brian has never acted more important than he was."

Brian's loyalty is legendary. In 1986, his former boss and strong supporter of C-SPAN, Bob Titsch, faced financial ruin. Even after selling his publishing business, his financial nest egg included little more than his wife's jewelry. Titsch's resolve to rebuild received only a slight boost from a talk with Brian and debilitating discouragement seemed ready to rule. A few days later, Titsch received an envelope from Brian with a note saying "Here's a check for $5,000. I don't care what happens to it. Use it to rebuild your empire. I believe in you and I know you can do it."[17] A personal check for $5,000 is significant for most people, but especially for Brian with his limited income and his frugality. Titsch remembers reading the note with overwhelming emotion, recognizing that "it was the biggest spiritual lift I ever got in my life. It gave me the strength to start over."[18] Titsch would go on to re-establish his publishing empire of over a dozen trade magazines.

Brian's loyalty to the cable industry runs deep. When the Cable Center opened on the campus of the University of Denver, Brian worried about making the facility a return destination, wondering what would draw people back after they visited the museum once. Offering C-SPAN's resources, he spearheaded the development of a series of videoconference courses linking students in Colorado with decision makers in Washington, D.C. The initiative eventually grew to include an even broader set of educational bridges with the addition of Pace (New York) and George Mason (Virginia) Universities.

MODEST NEEDS

In the Washington environment where status is measured by money and power, Brian has eschewed the typical perks of office. Brian's salary only recently topped $200,000, not a paltry sum, but nowhere near the salary of lesser positions at other networks. Brian says that a big salary increase "throws you off stride." His compensation package has been described as more like that of a small college president than a network executive.[19] Brian regularly fights attempts by his board members to raise his salary.

Although Brian comes off as bland and laid-back, his office belies some of his passions and human traits. Offices are often the outward expression of their occupants. The first impression of Brian's office is its location. He did not choose the premier site. One can peek through a large glass wall to see much of Brian's office. At first sight, it looks like a well-stocked library. On his computer is a picture of two old friends at a 60th birthday party. "One of them, crying with laughter, has a tissue up his nose."[20] It is as if Brian is grounded in his origins and old friends as he looks out over the city he has chosen to illuminate. The bookshelves also include a collection of twenty-seven replicas of Tweety Bird. There is a bit of whimsy in Brian when he admits that he is a Tweety buff. A bit sheepishly, he explains, "I just like him. Some people say I look a little bit like him."[21]

Despite being in Washington for close to forty years, Brian remains *in* Washington but not *of* Washington. Until recently, he lived in a modest townhouse in Arlington, Virginia. It was a bachelor "pad" without most of the accoutrements such a term implies.

While some argue that the way to a Washingtonian's heart runs through the hors d'oeuvre platter, the tactic holds little chance of success with Brian. Avoiding the Washington social scene, Brian would rather go home or stop in for some Thai food. About the most social Brian gets is at the C-SPAN Christmas party, "wantonly" shedding his conservative neck ware, he greets everyone heartily in his bright red tie.

His long and rather strange hours do not fit into the Washington party scene. Brian is rarely seen at dinner parties, embassy receptions, and other events "where contacts are forged or exploited."[22] He maintains a healthy skepticism of Washingtonians who always have an agenda, whether it is in the office during the day or on the cocktail circuit at night. As Brian sees it, "Here [in Washington,] everybody's going somewhere. They're ambitious, trying to control their image. And you can't have, very often, a genuine friendship with anybody in public life. You can't trust it."[23] Brian gets his grounding back home arguing, "I like Indiana better. I like the people better. I like the attitudes better. When I am not at work, I fall back on my old friends. I go back to my friends from Indiana, my original friends, because they are more genuine, down-to-earth. They're not angling for anything."[24]

Stories of Brian's personal frugality are legion. Never expect to find him traveling other than economy class. On the road, he rents the subcompact car and can't understand why people need a mid-size. Brian's yellow Toyota Corolla hatchback became a legend. He refused to give it up, even though many of his board members who "understand tangible things were embarrassed" when he picked them up at the airport. Brian still buys his country western music at Walmart. On the other hand, he presides over considerable institutional generosity. For the 1988 Republican presidential convention in New Orleans, the C-SPAN staff was unable to book rooms close to the convention site until the last minute. Faced with prepaid guarantees of their initial rooms, Brian did not hesitate to spend the extra $5,000 to make sure his people were safe and secure.

ON THE ROAD AGAIN

C-SPAN consultant and University of Maryland Professor John Splaine became a frequent traveling companion of Brian's. On the road he found him to "be very thoughtful, but when he wants to get going, it is time to get going." One morning in Lafayette, Indiana, after a talk at Purdue, Splaine recalls, "Brian set a departure time of 6:30. At 6:00 AM, I was in the middle of a bagel and Brian made it clear it was time to go without finishing breakfast. I pleaded, 'Can I finish my bagel?' and Brian answered pleasantly, but firmly, 'No, time to go.'" With a little guilt, Brian proceeded to load both their sets of luggage and got Splaine some food at the airport.

Whether out of Midwestern courtesy or the strategic desire to case a place out before a meeting, Brian always likes to be early. Splaine expresses with admiration, "I don't think he has ever been late to an interview in his life."

Brian loves frozen yogurt. He can spot a TCB store miles away. Splaine explains that he can drive by a shopping center and proclaim, "There must be a yogurt shop in there someplace. He would hone in on it and usually be right. One time, on the way to meet the mayor of Freeport, Illinois, they were both running behind schedule and in need of gas. Before I had finished filling the tank, Brian waved me off. He figured that saving the time from filling the tank would give them time for yogurt and they would still arrive early."

INNOCENTS ABROAD

The world has become accustomed to entertainment and political figures traveling with large entourages smoothing the way and making sure their employer picks up the right fork and fulfills local customs. Brian travels alone or with a friend, carrying his own bags and facing each new challenge with anticipation and innocence. At times, the origin of Brian's trips are as interesting as the trip itself.

As is often the case, new ideas at C-SPAN emerge from Brian's personal experiences. Time after time, *Booknote*'s guests referred to Alexis de Tocqueville as if everyone knew his contributions to American political thought. Brian admits, "I never lived in a very intellectual world" and suffered silent embarrassment. He finally decided, "I had to find out what Tocqueville was all about." In a first for *Booknotes*, Brian invited Alan Ryan, the author of the preface to a new publication of Tocqueville's *Democracy in America*. Armed with a better understanding of Tocqueville, Brian's brain floated around the idea of what to do with it. At an award ceremony recognizing C-SPAN's Lincoln-Douglas debate series, Brian answered the question of what C-SPAN would do next with the comment that they were considering reconstructing Tocqueville's trip around the country. After the ceremony, a young academic came up to him and mentioned he had visited Tocqueville's chateau in France. It did not take Brian long to decide that Tocqueville would best be understood by seeing his roots.

In preparation for a year-long set of programs following Alexis de Toqueville's 1831 visit to the United States, Brian traveled to France to visit Tocqueville's home. Finding himself in the wrong political party, Tocqueville secured a grant to study the penal system in the United States. Accompanied by his friend Gustave de Beaumont, he traveled around the country talking with a wide range of individuals. Early on, Tocqueville's fascination with prisons waned, setting the stage for his becoming one of the early "grant cheats." Leaving the prison project to Beaumont, Tocqueville focused his efforts on America's political and social character. His *Democracy in America* became a best seller, making Tocqueville very wealthy. Beaumont's fulfilling of the grant request resulted in a lengthy tome with little commercial value that gathered dust on the government agency shelves.

Brian's personal Tocqueville tour took him to Tocqueville's birthplace in Paris, the apartment he shared with Beaumont in Versailles, the village of Tocqueville, located in the Normandy region of France, near Cherbourg, roughly 225 miles from Paris.

The trip to the village of Tocqueville, with its three hundred residents, was to be highlighted by a visit to the family chateau-hosted visit with one of the writer's descendents, Count Guy d'Herouville. The adventure began with lunch in the village. Fearful of offending his host with too much garlic, Brian popped a stick of gum in his mouth. Walking through the garden, the diners were greeted by the count's large black dog. As they approached the château, Brian began searching for a place to dispose of his gum. Seeing no receptacle, he gave it a toss, only to have the dog intercept its trajectory. Now, Brian saw the large black dog running around with a big glob of white gum. He knew he "had to get that gum before anyone else sees it." He tried to discretely reach down with his right hand to remove it, but came away with a long string of gum and a patch of black hair. A similar maneuver with his left hand led to a similar result. With most of the gum gone and his hands filled with hair and gum, Brian entered the chateau to ponder the origin of Tocqueville's intellectual treatise.

THE PERSONAL COSTS OF SUCCESS

In the demanding schedule of keeping C–SPAN going, Brian had missed seeing his father the last few weeks of his life. As his mother's cancer worsened, the stars aligned, allowing him to play both good son and good corporate executive. Brian is good to his word and tries to balance all his responsibilities. When his mother's health was failing from brain cancer, Brian made a trip back to Indiana and agreed to make fifteen speeches and teach a class. In the middle of this flurry of activity, the dutiful son took his mother to the hospital and was with her when she died. The activity probably was good medicine for taking his mind off the grave situation. Once it was all over, he remembers that, "It hit me like a ton of bricks." When she lapsed into a coma, Brian felt he could depart. On an early morning trip to the airport, he made a final stop at the hospital. As he walked into his mother's hospital room, the team of nurses looked up and Brian saw his mother take her last breath. One nurse said in a comforting tone, "She waited for you."

SPATS, SQUABBLES, AND SHORTCOMINGS

In a town where people are known by the enemies they make, Brian's slate of enemies remains pretty short and tepid. He has little time for CBS commentator Andy Rooney, who attacked him personally at a society of Professional Journalists roast of Walter Cronkite. Rooney commented, "Brian Lamb worked for the Nixon-Agnew White House and we know what Nixon and Agnew thought of the First Amendment."[25] Brian saw it as an uninformed "cheap shot." In the battle over public funding for public television, Bill Moyers explained Speaker Newt Gingrich's attack on public television on C-SPAN by pointing out that C-SPAN "is the creature of the cable industry, run by friends of the new speaker of the House."[26] In writing the history of public television, James Ledbetter again used guilt by association to hang the albatross around Brian's neck by attempting to improve upon Moyer's volley and say, "He might have added that the man interviewing Gingrich, C-SPAN founder Brian Lamb, had been an aide to Clay Whitehead when the Nixon administration tried to shut down public broadcasting."[27] Brian will probably go to the grave with the words "who once worked for Richard Nixon" indelibly associated with his name and available for any critic to troop out to explain any shortcoming.

Within Congress and among his interview subjects, it is hard to find anyone who questions Brian's motives or wishes him ill. The two exceptions would be former congressman Charlie Rose and his previous wife, Joan Teague, who probably still smart from Brian's success in battles with them over controlling House broadcasting.

Brian has pretty thick skin when criticisms are either partially valid or humorous. His strong sense of who he is allows him to accept what some would see as self-image, destructing criticisms. Impersonators of him on *Saturday Night Live* create minimal angst. As Brian puts it, "I've been described as a test pattern without color. . . . They call me dull, stupid, bald. As long as we are delivering the mission, it goes with the territory."[28]

In a town where strengths are inflated and weaknesses hidden, Lamb is refreshingly honest trotting out his own personal demons with little hesitancy. When asked about his own shortcomings, he admits that "I have been accused of having a short attention span. . . . I sometimes jump to conclusions, when if I waited a little bit longer, I'll find out that my first instincts weren't right. . . . I have to fight cynicism, based on being in Washington for 40 years. It's a constant fight."[29]

Brian has a modest view of himself, willingly telling how he compensates. No magic remedy appears. Hard work and diligence in reading and marking up everyone of the over eight hundred books featured on *Booknotes* prepared him to carry out unparalleled interviews. Brian makes the best personal use of his time, recognizing the need to bow to one's body clock. There are clearly "morning people," and "night people," who do their best and most productive work at different times of the day. Trying to work against one's body clock leads to unproductive frustration. Brian explains his quirky hours of being in bed by 8:00 and up at 3:00 to read by saying, "The best thing about the middle of the night is it's quiet. A lot of things I'm not: I'm not an intellectual, I'm not a scholar and I'm not a speed reader. I just love to learn."[30] About the only compliment he readily gives himself is that "my curiosity level is higher than most people, but I am really of average intellect and average knowledge, and so, when I ask a question, I'm asking for the average person."[31] Brian's curiosity is reflected in his reading habits that stem from the desire to "find out before anyone else. I want to know before someone says, 'Did you hear?'"[32] He gets up early to read books. Arriving at the office at 6:30, he reads over a half dozen newspapers and takes a look at the Drudge Report.

FOCUS ON THE BRIDGE

In a media world filled with superstars sporting $200 blow dry haircuts of their Grecian Formula locks, Brian stands out from his ordinariness. He is less than six feet, round-faced, with a head of increasingly thinning gray hair. No one tunes in to comment on his wardrobe. His starched white shirt, conservative tie, and dark blue suit are virtually indistinguishable from one day to the next. His low-key manner and boring wardrobe almost scream, "It is not about me!" The electronic media almost demands stardom. From the earliest eras, well-known personalities added legitimacy to the news. Radio's Gabriel Heeter endeared himself to listeners with a welcome phrase that became his famous trademark: "Ah, yes, I've got good news tonight!" Virtually everybody who listened to the radio recognized Lowell Thomas' "Good evening, everybody" and his sign-off, "So long, until tomorrow." Edward R. Murrow captivated his radio and later television audience with "Good night and good luck." Murrow expanded his following by producing news specials and by hosting "Person to Person," where he brought television cameras into the homes of public officials and stars. Walter Cronkite became the most trusted person in America by assuring people that "and that's the way it is." More contemporary news stars are promoted by the names of their programs:

> "CBS Evening News with Katie Couric"
> "NBC Evening News with Brian Williams"
> "World News with Charles Gibson"

When one of the anchors is physically missing, the aura of their name remains as a disembodied voice or on-screen crawl announcing, "Filling in for Katie Couric tonight is." From the titles, one gets the feeling that without

Couric, Williams, or Gibson, there would be no news. Is there a graphic already developed saying, "Sorry, due to the sickness of our anchor, no news happened today. Tune in tomorrow to see if the news has returned."

News anchors in the commercial media increasingly get out from behind their desks to collect and report news themselves. From high visibility interviews with world celebrities (such as Dan Rather and Saddam Hussein) to visits to natural disasters and war zones, news media stars promise to bring the important news directly to us. News production typically uses "crawls" identifying the newsperson and encouraging a personal relationship with them. Pollsters often find that respondents can't identify the network they watch, but can tell them *who* they watch.

Countering this trend, Brian is proud of the fact that he has never uttered his name on the air and does not identify himself or other hosts. Callers have to be pretty media savvy to know Brian, and it is almost like an inside joke when they call him by name. When callers mention his name, Brian skips over the familiarity, almost embarrassed by the attention.

Although C-SPAN hosts follow a regular schedule, it is never publicly announced and their names only slip out on the tongues of guests. If a change in hosts is necessary due to sickness or scheduling, not a big deal is made of the shift. C-SPAN hosts are interchangeable pegs on a board, making no distinction on status.

A GRAVE BRIDGE TO THE PAST

One of Brian's most interesting passions, or perhaps obsessions, is the commitment to visit every presidential and vice-presidential gravesite, recording the event by having his picture taken. During three of his visits, there was no one else around to validate his presence, so Brian went ahead and held the camera out to take his own picture in front of the graves, before shooting a picture of the grave itself. When asked why someone would do such a thing as visiting graves, Brian answers, "That's how 'C' students learn. You go and see for yourself."[33] The idea of the visits came during a *Booknotes* interview with historian Richard Norton Smith who explained he had begun his own gravesite visit odyssey at age nine. Something clicked in Brian's mind and he said, "I'm going to do that." He brought the camera along to prove to Richard Norton Smith that he had done it.[34]

Brian not only got hooked on the idea, but stepped up the pace, completing his personal quest in eighteen months. Not only has he visited every presidential gravesite, but has written a book about it. He explains that visiting graves is great "for tourists like you and me who get a kick out of learning through personal experience." In most cases, the visits were solitary and decorous, but Brian's frugality and passion lured him from his law-abiding path. One weekend he planned a triple-hitter, visiting three gravesites in two days. Setting out for Albany, New York, in a rented car to chalk-up the gravesite of Chester A. Arthur, Brian found himself spotting his prey on the other side of cemetery gates that had been closed at 5:00 PM. He figured, "I'd come too far to miss it. Spying no one, I climbed the cemetery's stone fence, still dressed in my business suit. Thankfully, I was able to find the grave, pay my respects, and snap a few photos without being spotted."[35] Keeping both his frugality and the personal nature of his pursuit, Brian took virtually all of the pictures in his presidential gravesite book with his own "point-and-shoot" 35-mm camera.

In a second "crime spree," Brian went in pursuit of a picture of Robert Frost's Cabin in Vermont. Setting out camera in hand and using directions provided by Jay Parini on *Booknotes*, he located the path to Frost's cabin near Middlebury, Vermont. Coming face-to-face with a prominent "No Trespassing" sign failed to dissuade him. "Figuring that any owner would conclude that a business-suited traveler who had flown in from Washington and driven two hours just to find this spot meant no harm, I decided to ignore the sign. I walked down the leafy path—exactly the kind Frost describes in his poetry—found the cabin, and took my shot."[36]

Encouraging others to follow his footsteps, Brian preaches "The sites, which are often near boyhood homes or family estates, offer a glimpse into the making and mind-set of the men who became president. They also offer a powerful reminder of the limitation of seeking power and fame."[37] One of the key lessons you learn "is that no matter how powerful you are, you will die, and there's nothing that power can do to stop it."[38] The visits however, "aren't so much about death as they are about personal and political symbolism."[39]

As an encore, Lamb has visited every vice-presidential gravesite, except for Nelson Rockefeller, who is buried on private property. He has even written to the Rockefeller family requesting access.

CREATING A PAPER BRIDGE

Fascinated by the process of writing, Brian marshaled his time and efforts to better understand, and eventually participate in, the process. *Booknotes* interviews served his own fascination, not only with interesting ideas, but they also gave him the opportunity to delve into the experiences of successful writers. He regularly asked how authors got the ideas for their books, how they actually went about writing, and how they got the book published. His service on the Borders board of directors allowed him to better understand the retail side of publishing. In recognizing the importance of ethics in public life, Brian resigned from the Borders board in 1997, saying that with "C-SPAN's recent expansion of its book-related programs has led me to conclude that it is no longer appropriate for me to serve as a director of a bookseller."[40]

The love affair with books eventually led Brian to become an author. His first book, *C-SPAN: America's Town Hall*, profiled C-SPAN users. *Booknotes: America's Finest Authors of Reading, Writing, and the Power of Ideas* focused on the writing process. His conclusions were encouraging to writers, indicating that there was no one pattern for success. He found the author's stories so compelling he wanted to share them with a broader audience by turning them into a book.

Brian launched his own foray into the world of authorship like a businessman, delegating one of his staff to pick the minds of book publicists. They were frank about the fact that Brian's name, with his "charisma and following, still might not be sexy enough."[41] The publicists suggested that a book emanating from *Booknotes* needed to be filled with "juicy tidbits . . . information never before revealed to the public . . . insights into behind the scenes interchange between Brian and the authors."[42] Nothing could be further from the C-SPAN approach of taking viewers directly behind the scenes, not simply giving them interpreted glimpses of Brian as an insider. Brian and his staff marched forward with a C-SPAN type of book, which largely included uncut portions of interviews where authors described the intellectual and mechanical aspects of their writing.

Brian's own writing approach resembles that of the corporate executive. He comes up with the basic idea, and delegates a great deal of the research and writing to his staff. Although Brian's name features prominently on each book, undoubtedly out of commercial considerations pressed by the publishers, Brian is quite generous in acknowledging the significant contribution made by staff members. Utilizing his hobby, Brian took twenty-nine of the forty-one pictures in his first *Booknotes* book.

BOOKNOTES' WRITERS ON WRITING

- Civil War historian Shelby Foote writes with a dip pen, claiming it slows him down and lets him think about every word he puts down.
- Presidential historian Forrest McDonald prefers writing longhand in the nude on his isolated porch, with his wife transcribing and editing finished pages.
- Historian Doris Kearns Goodwin writes longhand sitting on a couch before putting the text in a computer.
- Columnist George Will stuck with his pen until a broken arm forced him to move to the computer for writing.
- Writer Christopher Hitchens prefers to write on his laptop at a Dupont Circle bar.
- Former school principal Madeline Cartwright wrote her critique of American education on her computer, sitting on her bed with her grandchildren jumping up and down.
- CBS reporter Charles Kuralt rented a small writing office, decorating it "with the feel of a seedy, failing, small gentleman's club."

Source: Brian Lamb. 1997. *Booknotes: America's Finest Authors of Reading, Writing, and the Power of Ideas*. New York: Times Books.

BOOKS BY BRIAN LAMB

- *C-SPAN Town Hall*
- *Booknotes: America's Finest Authors of Reading, Writing, and the Power of Ideas*
- *Life Stories: Notable Biographers on the People Who Shaped America*
- *Booknotes: Stories from American History*
- *Booknotes on American Character: People, Politics, and Conflict in American History*
- *Who is Buried in Grant's Tomb?*

PRAISING THE BRIDGE, NOT THE BRIDGE BUILDER

Brian is seemingly embarrassed by personal accolades. If he had a trophy case in his office, an almost impossible thing to conceive, it would be overflowing with the hundreds of awards C-SPAN has received. There is no "ego wall" with his honorary degrees or awards. When C-SPAN receives awards, he likes to send other staff members to accept them, even though the organization giving the award wants "the" man. A small selection of awards is displayed in the entryway to all offices, a not so subtle message to staff and visitors that they belong to everyone on the staff.

Brian's modesty almost glows with depreciation. It is hard to get him to accept personal credit for almost anything.

When asked about his high school radio program, "Dance Date," he comments, "Great name isn't it? About as good as C-SPAN. I invented both of those names and never liked either one of them."[43]

On air, Brian's discomfort with adulation looms even larger. He looked particularly uncomfortable when a caller broke two "rules" of using his name on the air and praising him by saying "Brian, in Japan they have a tradition of naming extremely important individuals as 'national treasures.' If the U.S. were to institute such a policy, the first person to be so honored should be Brian Lamb."[44]

No doubt Brian cringes at some of the adulations he receives. Lobbyist and former Tip O'Neill aide Gary Hymel practically has the sculptors poised with their tools when he says, "Brian has brought democracy to the people of America—he's up there with Jefferson and Lincoln and the greats."

Brian has always been uncomfortable with personal publicity. After a rather detailed article ran in the *New Yorker*,[45] Brian told his staff, "This is it. . . . I am not going to get into my personal life. There is more to C-SPAN than just Brian Lamb."

Descriptions of C-SPAN border on unadulterated adulation. Callers often preface their comments with, "Thank God for C-SPAN." Chris Matthews, CNBC host of "Hardball" and former Capitol Hill aide to then-Speaker Tip O'Neill got into a game of one-upmanship with then-Wyoming Senator Alan Simpson over Lamb. When Simpson argued, "Brian Lamb deserves the Congressional Medal of Honor for sticking with it through think and thin." Matthews countered with, "I think he deserves the Medal of Freedom." Just to lay the competition to rest, Matthews trumped the categories by saying, "I think Brian Lamb is God. . . . He's nonpartisan, and he's brought Congress in its present form to the American people. It took tremendous patriotism to do that."[46] Lamb is typically much more modest and probably cringed at the interchange. He describes C-SPAN as "a social good" and a "public service." When asked if C-SPAN has been good for America, Lamb displays some admirable Midwestern candor, "I have trouble answering," Lamb admits, "I don't want to sound self-serving. I don't know."[47]

While Brian carries out his interviews to inform the American public, he revels in the fact that he constantly learns himself. Dixon, Illinois, the Birthplace of Ronald Reagan and Lafayette, Indiana, are only 160 miles apart physically, but much closer in temperament and outlook. Sitting across from Ronald Reagan in the Oval Office, Brian noticed a plaque that said: "There's no limit to what a man can do or where he can go if he doesn't mind who gets the credit." Lamb admits, "I've used that. I just find it to be incredibly important."[48] When C-SPAN turned twenty-five, he publicly attempted to deflect some of the adulation by giving significant credit to Janet Fay, the first C-SPAN employee.

Taking Reagan's principle a bit further, Brian thrilled his graduation audience at Illinois's Knox College. Graduation speakers by tradition and by expectation are positioned on high platforms and become the focal point for the crowd. The speech becomes a preface for the honorary degree the speaker really desires. While few of us can remember who spoke at our graduation and even fewer can remember what they said, some extraterrestrial anthropologist watching this strange tribal ritual would probably write back that the event was designed to honor the person who monopolized the microphone for the longest period. Brian's discomfort with notoriety propelled him to take an action remembered by much of the Knox College crowd in 2000. He began his speech by taking out a pocket-sized still camera and focused it on the graduates, promising to make the pictures available to the graduates on the C-SPAN website.[49] That simple act served as a dramatic reminder this was their day, not his.

STAFF AFFECTION

Some organizations cherry-pick staff members with particular skills able to hit the ground running. Corporate headhunters, who lure star performers laterally from competing entities, typically recruit top-level staff members. Largely out of necessity, Brian's hiring has focused more on commitment than proven competence. Low salaries, long hours, and a shaky future discouraged lateral transfers. In the early years, Brian hired promising young applicants, watched them perform, and promoted from within. Many in the mid- and upper-levels of the operation say, "I never expected or intended to do this kind of a job." Brian's staff appreciates both his guidance and the leeway provided. They talk about him "stretching me in ways I didn't know I could go." As one staff member put it, "Brian made me who I am. I was molded like a piece of clay. He saw my talents and helped me develop them. He imbued me with his principles in a kind but forceful way."

Brian's loyalty to his staff and providing them opportunities to move upward, lead to a very stable employee pool. Few employees leave C-SPAN. While not universal, it is common for staff to admit, "What a great job. I wake up every morning excited about doing something important."

PAYBACK

Outside the halls of C-SPAN, Brian has increasingly become the public face of C-SPAN, with an active speaking scheduled. Unlike most people who have "made it," Brian refuses to accept an honorarium, viewing the trips as a "payback tour" helping out those who helped C-SPAN in the past. Following Brian around on the speaking circuit reinforces the view of a person driven by curiosity. He hopes to learn more about his audience than they learn about him. He likes to arrive early, shake hands with as many of the audience members as possible, and store their names and hometowns in his memory bank. He loves to blow the audience away by personalizing his comments using the names and information tidbits about individuals in front of him. It is more than a parlor trick or an activity he engages in for effect. The more important object lies in explaining the driving force behind journalism. Brian drives the point home saying, "Curiosity is the only thing that leads to journalism."[50]

A typical Brian Lamb speech reflects his confidence in the audience to ask the right questions. A brief introduction slides quickly into a question-and-answer session. With a small group, he quickly turns it into an interview and, unless the audience is clever, Brian will fully control the information flow.

MEASURING SUCCESS

Brian recognizes that C-SPAN will never appeal to everyone. In many ways, it is a great relief that C-SPAN does not have to fight the ratings game with other networks. C-SPAN has no advertising and receives its funding from the cable industry no matter the size or demographics of its audience.

He modestly concludes that C-SPAN "matters to a certain slice of the American public. I call them the 10-percenters. I call them the junkies."[51]

Brian has become a spokesman for open government not only in the United States but worldwide, making presentations to parliaments in Israel and France. The C-SPAN offices have become a prime destination for parliamentarians and their staffs from numerous countries. Brian is always the gracious host, sharing his knowledge and experiences. There is one major exception. No matter the audience, Brian hedges on answering the question, "What has the impact of C-SPAN been?" It comes up in almost every speech or public session in which Brian is involved. Whether out of modesty, political care, or actual lack of an opinion, he generally sidesteps the question with skill.

The closest he comes to assessing impact is to point out how C-SPAN has expanded access to the public consciousness. In the early 1990s, when Bill Clinton was president and the Republicans controlled Congress, Brian pointed out, "People have begun to see that there is not just one human being running this country. You have a Speaker now who is so active and an activist . . . and he has equal access on the television screen . . . equal access, that's what's different."[52]

THE COOL ENIGMA

On the other hand, Brian proclaims, "I am not a wonk. Wonks spend their lives on public policy. I'm fascinated by what makes it all work, but I have no great plan for America."[53] Brian is a sought after speaker, especially to college audiences, more for where he came from then for where he is going. He readily continually admits to being a 'C' student at Purdue, wearing it more as a badge of honor than as a mark of mediocrity. He appeals to other 'C' students in his audience that what you show interest in and where you place your efforts at one time in your life does not doom you to perpetually remain at that level of understanding and performance. Simply, his message boils down to the argument that anyone can do great things if led by their passions and willing to work hard.

LOOKING BACK OVER THE BRIDGE

While the network is self-consciously anti-personality and Lamb is genuinely self-effacing, there would be no C-SPAN without his vision and efforts. A modest Midwesterner from Indiana, Lamb eschews personal promotion and the star system of modern media. He cooperates with the media when it attempts to understand what he is doing, but always tries to redirect the interest to C-SPAN, rather than profiling himself as a persona. His discomfort with this biography did not seem like false modesty, but rather fear that a change in his personal approach to becoming a focus of any activity would unleash a plague of personality on the network. He realizes the temptation of stardom, but recognizes its shallow roots. Just as the discoverer of the genie's bottle might wish for a million dollars for himself and a million dollars for his worst enemy, most of us assume we can handle good fortune and our enemies cannot. Brian does not want to tempt his successors. Brian honestly wants to avoid the domination of C-SPAN by personalities, including his own. He is uncomfortable with the media attention paid to him as an individual. It is hard to think of C-SPAN and not think about Brian Lamb. Even his staff tends to explain C-SPAN philosophy and approaches by interchangeably using the terms "he" and "C-SPAN."

9

MAINTAINING THE BRIDGE

It is the nature of a man as he grows older, a small bridge in
time, to protest against change, particularly change for the
better.

—John Steinbeck (1902–1968),
Travels with Charley: In Search of America, 1962

THE ARCHITECT ON THE MAINTENANCE CREW

Through normal attrition, founding fathers drop by the wayside, leaving
their creations to continue on their own. In some organizations,
founders stay around too long, handcuffing organizations to outdated
modes of behavior and stifling growth. As the father of C-SPAN, Brian
seems to have discovered a good way to capitalize on the advantages of having the founding father still on site without having the organization fall victim to the potential dangers.

One of Brian's key contributions lies in serving as a subtle cheerleader
for the C-SPAN mission and the personal joy staff members gain buying
into it. The polar opposite of late-career burnout, he carries with him
much of the same thrill he had on the first day of C-SPAN's existence. In
the tone of a child anticipating Christmas, he declares, "The excitement I
get when I get that glimpse of some world that I wouldn't ever get [with-
out C-SPAN] is still there today."[1]

NO WEAK EFFORTS

Many organizations pass down their goals and principles in a brief pamphlet or allow informal osmosis to permeate employee consciousness. Few organizations commit the kind of resources C-SPAN does to passing on its goals and principles to its staff. Relatively new employees are pulled off their jobs for "C-SPAN Week" and attend an intensive set of seminars on C-SPAN's mission. Not only does someone have to cover for the employee learning the C-SPAN mantra, but key employees, from Brian on down, also take time from their jobs to orient the "newbies" and bring them into the fold.

The creation of C-SPAN Week was pure genius. The very fact that staff members would be given a week off their jobs to develop a broad view of C-SPAN and absorb its mission in and of itself reveals Brian's priority of having a team where everyone sings from the same page. Such orientations can come too early, before individuals know their jobs or possess enough information to ask questions. The goal of C-SPAN Week is to get people to buy into the idea of C-SPAN. It is generally not a tough sell. Individuals gravitate to C-SPAN with some sense of its mission. Above and beyond cheerleading and preaching to the choir, the sessions tackle issues of what to cover and how to cover it in a C-SPAN manner. Effective organizations learn from their mistakes. An important part of C-SPAN Week emerges from identifying, diagnosing, and proposing solutions to on-screen errors. Little things make a big difference. Although C-SPAN staff members don't have their names on the screen, public officials and guests do. Misspelling a name not only undermines the ego of the person on-screen, but also diminishes the legitimacy of all C-SPAN coverage. An irrelevant cut-away shot comes as a shock to regular C-SPAN viewers accustomed to viewing events through a focus on official action. Thus, a member of the team running the character generator for names or in charge of the backup camera needs to realize the importance of his or her role in the end product.

PROTECTING THE BRIDGE

Probably more than anyone will ever know, Brian's life and self-esteem are invested in C-SPAN. It is his baby, conceived, brought into the world, nurtured, and now protected by all his psychic and physical energy. For over 25 years it was his wife, family, and mistress. Only in the last few years, has he been weaned from its constant demands—if just a little. He is fiercely protective. He battles with Congress for control of the cameras, with the cable operators to protect C-SPAN from commercialization, and with the government over public policies that would undermine C-SPAN's mission.

One staff member, frustrated with his experience with commercial television, points out, "Brian is a true visionary, who knows what he wants. He does not get caught in the mechanics. He sees new technology as a way to fulfill C-SPAN's mission." Succeeding waves of technology are viewed less as challenges than opportunities to present the product more effectively to more people. In many ways, "Brian is one of the founders of the information age, always thinking one step ahead for applications of new technology." Brian found ways to utilize cable television, satellite radio, websites, and digital television well before most information providers. For Brian, new technology stands as "add-on enhancements" for C-SPAN's basic product. While some media see new technologies as replacements, Brian forces C-SPAN to "stick with its knitting," making sure it remains true to its initial goal before venturing out.

In his initial negotiations with the cable industry, Brian cut a deal in which cable operators guaranteed C-SPAN funding, whether or not they broadcast its programming. In the early years, satellite capacity exceeded programming and little conflict developed. As new cable channels developed and kicked back advertising revenue, using a channel for C-SPAN meant giving up revenue. While Brian has always been proud that C-SPAN does not rely on ratings, programming without a delivery mechanism means little.

The situation became more difficult when Congress considered "must-carry" legislation, requiring cable systems to include programming from the major commercial networks. Brian exhibited his frustration in saying, "My attitude is one of controlled rage. The government writes a piece of legislation that sounded good, but it is the public service channel that is being hardest hit." Even after the results of "must carry" became evident, Brian still philosophically opposed plans to require C-SPAN carriage. In his words, "The Congress has done severe damage to this network, and there is no way to change that without doing us a special favor, which we don't want." Although some proposed legislating C-SPAN coverage, special treatment was not in Brian's vocabulary. Sensing great danger, Brian reluctantly stepped over the line from observer to participant to testify in Congress. As numerous cable systems planned to drop or cut back C-SPAN coverage, Brian relied on his skill in convincing his board to persuade their colleagues and called on the audience to put pressure on their local cable systems. In most cases, the cutbacks were stemmed.

PUBLIC RELATIONS

Thousands of hours behind the mike listening to phone calls have been an education for Brian. Far from being disillusioned, he regularly argues both on and off the air that "the public is much smarter than the politicians give them credit for." Listing to the callers is affirming rather than discouraging. He concludes, "I'm actually not surprised by the breadth of the callers. I came from a small town in Indiana, and I was interested in all this because I knew my viewers were interested and they weren't sophisticated policy wonks, and I've always thought the average person . . . could deal with all this as well as anybody else."[2] He feels, "There's always been a difference in the way people in Washington think about an issue and the way it's done in the rest of the country. What Washington will tolerate, more and more, the rest of the country will not." Thinking and tolerating depend on understanding and knowing. Lacking the link provided by C-SPAN, the public corrective remains an ineffective medicine.

C-SPAN cannot claim huge audiences, but it does draw political "movers and shakers" who use C-SPAN as ammunition in their political battles. Brian subscribes to a "wave factor" to explain how news stories spread through the listening and viewing audiences. Hosts and callers on one program spread shreds of information mentioned on other programs. With each repetition the credibility of the message increases. The validity of an idea stems from "who" repeated it and how often it is repeated. This "escalation of validation" can build a wall around misinformation and makes it difficult to challenge. In studying small groups, Irving Janis found similar processes underlying what he called "group-think."[3] Information and misinformation can each have their believability enhanced by repetition. The speed of electronic information transfer and multiple outlets reduce the ability of anyone to check the validity of a story before disseminating it further. In the previous print era, editors and reporters checked the validity of stories to protect their institution's professional credibility and fear from lawsuits. The anonymity of call-in participants, and the lack of well-established expectations that the host will serve as a credibility check, undermine the potential for holding anyone accountable for the spread of misinformation. Apocryphal exaggerations or just plain lies can quickly be elevated to the position of absolute truths. Brian's goal for C-SPAN begins with broadcasting full events and allowing the audience to add their own interpretations. Additionally, Brian and other hosts regularly ask, "Where did you get that information?"

Brian generally praises call-in participants in public, while reflecting a more sanguine view in his more unguarded moments. During one heated exchange where a caller implied Brian's culpability with the misdeeds of some Washington players since he was "friends with these people," Brian asserted, "Callers say the most ridiculous things I have ever heard in my life, but we don't say that [on the air]." He, of course had just said that on the air.[4]

HOOKING ANOTHER GENERATION OF JUNKIES

Using the C-SPAN Foundation as the destination of his book revenues and budgeted funds, Brian seeks to introduce a new generation of viewers to C-SPAN. The two C-SPAN buses visit schools around the country with a full production studio and opportunities to interact with C-SPAN content. An educational website and conferences introduce students and teachers to what C-SPAN can contribute to education. Contests aimed at high school students attempt to hook them on C-SPAN early and implant C-SPAN viewing as a lifelong, carryover "sport." If a program can be presented as contributing to a C-SPAN educational mission, Brian is an easy sell.

In many ways Brian is a throwback to the era when radio dominated the media scene. He remembers radio as his first taste of excelling on his own. He always assumed that radio would be his life, a worthy aspiration for someone who still believes that "radio has a lot more magic than TV." At one point, he and his brother thought about buying a radio station in Belfast, Maine. The $87,000 price tag was less intimidating than the realization that one or both of them would have to work the station on a day-to-day basis. Later, when a radio station became available in Washington, D.C., Brian pushed C-SPAN to get into the radio business, taking the C-SPAN format into another medium. When digital radio came along, Brian was quick to urge its usage.

BUILDING NEW LANES AND UPGRADING THE BRIDGE

Brian serves as the point man for expanding C-SPAN access to a broader range of public affairs events. The battles go on in public and private. In his fights for public access, he is a realist, recognizing that "control is the number-one word used in this town—controlling one's image."[5] Permitting cameras at speeches or meetings has the potential to catch unscripted comments, embarrassing slips of the tongue, or unflattering pictures.

Brian's continuing challenge to the leaders of political institutions expresses a basic trust in the public and their ability to make reasoned judgments about phenomenon. He asserted that "people in an open society do not demand infallibility from their institutions, but it is difficult for them to accept what they are prohibited from observing."[6] The idea is not original. Lord Acton, the nineteenth-century British historian, asserted, "Everything secret denigrates, even the administration of justice; nothing is safe that does not show how it can bear discussion and publicity."[7] In the international realm, President Woodrow Wilson argued for "open covenants of peace, openly arrived at" as part of his Fourteen Points.

COURTING COVERAGE

True friendship is a rare commodity in politics. The dictum that "politics makes strange bedfellows," not only describes a strategy of coalition building, but also implies that today's friends are tomorrow's opponents. In such an environment, there is a great temptation to see acquaintances from the perspective of "use them and then lose them," or "prop them up and then drop them." Brian's goal to get C-SPAN cameras into the highest courts of the land brings him into direct conflict with one of his old friends, Justice Antonin Scalia (who he calls "Nino"), with whom he worked in the Nixon administration's Office of Telecommunications Policy. The young lawyer and public relations man used to work out strategies over Scalia's kitchen table. The friendship extends beyond the superficial, with Brian serving as the godfather of Scalia's son, Matthew. Brian points out that, "I've known him very well. I've been in his home many times—and I totally disagree with almost everything he says about cameras."[8] Scalia not only has opposed cameras in the courtroom, but has also refused to allow C-SPAN to broadcast his speeches. Not mincing words, Brian asserts, "The camera should go into the Supreme Court, but over David Souter's dead body, or over Nino Scalia's dead body. Cameras should go anywhere there's a public event."[9] Brian and Scalia parried in public over the issue, with Brian remembering, "I scourged him pretty well in public. It may have ticked him off, but I don't think there is any grudge. There was no duplicity. If we disagreed in public over the issue, the disagreement in private was even stronger." The friendship, however, remains intact. He respects Scalia as "dogmatic, but honest about it." Unlike many assumptions about the personal side of Washington, Lamb asserts, "while it is fun to personally know a Supreme Court Justice, it is absolutely no benefit to me in my job."

Brian separates his policy disagreement with Scalia from their friendship. He recognizes it as a strain, but not enough of one to jettison a thirty-year relationship. Well after a series of skirmishes with Brian, Scalia showed up at an award ceremony where Brian received the National Archives "Records of Achievement Award," explaining simply, "I'm an FOB— Friend of Brian."[10]

THE WINDOW ON CONGRESS

Each change of leadership in Congress finds Brian knocking on the door or, perhaps more aptly, standing outside the door trying to pry it open. At a time in one's life when many remain satisfied in resting on their laurels, Brian continues to push his dream forward. He lost no time in pouncing on Speaker-designate Nancy Pelosi (D-CA) after the Democrats took control of the House after the 2006 elections. When she promised to preside over a House that is "the most honest and open in history,"[11] Brian saw an opening. His plea was simple, if revolutionary. "Let C-SPAN in." Reversing almost a quarter century of televising rules, Brian's letter asked for the right to control the cameras, rather than the House staff under control of the speaker. He argued that the current system "does a disservice to the institution and to the public. You can never get a reaction shot. Fixed cameras take "out of the experience any of the soul" or sense of give and take.[12] The shift in camera control would give the average viewer "the same access as any citizen who's watching the debate while sitting in the House gallery" (see textbox). Speaker Pelosi rejected the plea, arguing that the "dignity and decorum of the United States House of Representatives are best preserved by maintaining the current system of televised proceedings." Although losing the battle, Brian again went on record for open government in the hope of wearing down the opposition in the longer war.

A PUBLIC SERVICE CREATED
BY AMERICA'S CABLE
TELEVISION COMPANIES

Brian P. Lamb
Chairman and Chief Executive Officer

December 14, 2006

Hon. Nancy Pelosi
Speaker-Designate
US House of Representatives
Washington, DC 20515

Dear Representative Pelosi:

After your party's November 16th leadership elections, you held a news conference in which you pledged to lead a congress committed to openness. In that spirit and as you and your leadership team work through the many organizational decisions needed for the 110th Congress, we'd like to make two requests of you which we were unsuccessful in pursuing with the incoming Republican majority twelve years ago:

- Allow House floor proceedings to be covered by C-SPAN cameras.

- Release individual House votes electronically immediately after voting periods have closed

Independent media cameras have long been permitted in congressional committees, yet for nearly 30 years, television cameras in the House chamber have operated under the control of the Speaker. This compromise was crafted long ago to convince wary members to allow congressional sessions to be televised, and in the ensuing years it has become an anachronism that does a disservice to the institution and to the public. During debate, congressional technicians are limited to taking static, head-on shots of the representative who's speaking at the podium. Rules and established practices prevent congressional cameras from taking individual reaction shots or from panning the chamber, leaving viewers with an incomplete picture of what's happening in the House of Representatives.

For a dozen years or more, independent media cameras have been permitted in the House chamber during joint sessions and joint meetings. We're asking you to take the next step and open the regular House floor proceedings to C-SPAN cameras on a permanent basis. We will commit to covering House debate in the same manner we televise congressional hearings—fully, accurately, and with the unbiased production style on which we've built our reputation for the past 28 years. We also pledge to make our floor coverage fully available to accredited news media following established pool practices.

Immediate electronic access to voting records is also an important step in making the House more open and accessible to the television viewing public. Votes have been electronically recorded for decades. A visitor to the chamber can watch as they are recorded in real-time on an electronic tally board. Yet, official public release of individual votes is still delivered long after a vote has closed. Frequently, by the time individual voting records are released by the Clerk, the House has moved on to other issues. The net effect is that this important information is rarely included in C-SPAN's live telecasts of House floor proceedings. Members' votes are the most critical part of Congress' public record. Help us present a complete picture of Congress' work by permitting immediate electronic release of individual votes.

Both of these proposals are made with one simple goal in mind—to allow a viewer of C-SPAN's gavel-to-gavel coverage the same access to information as any citizen who's watching the debate while sitting in the House gallery.

On March 19, 1979, when the House was televised for the first time, Representative Al Gore made a speech on the floor that welcomed Congress to the television age. He predicted that members would become so comfortable with the presence of television that they would soon move to open the floor proceedings to coverage by the independent media.

Under your leadership, Speaker-designate Pelosi, we hope that Al Gore's long ago prediction will finally become reality. Please let us know what we can do to advance your consideration of these two important requests.

Sincerely,

Brian P. Lamb
Chairman and CEO

Cc: Hon. Steny Hoyer
        Hon. John Boehner

NANCY PELOSI
8TH DISTRICT, CALIFORNIA
DEMOCRATIC LEADER

H–204, THE CAPITOL
WASHINGTON, DC 20515–653

One Hundred Eighth Congress
U.S. House of Representatives
Office of the Democratic Leader

December 22, 2006

Mr. Brian P. Lamb
Chairman and Chief Executive Officer
C-SPAN
400 North Capitol Street
Washington, D.C. 20001

Dear Mr. Lamb:

Thank you for your thoughtful letter in which you ask that C-SPAN be permitted to cover House floor proceedings with its own cameras and that the House release individual House votes electronically immediately after voting periods have closed. I have asked the Clerk of the House to consider the latter request and report to the House Leadership on whether such a release is technically feasible and, if so, whether it can be accomplished in a manner that preserves the accuracy of the vote tally.

As to your first request, I believe that the dignity and decorum of the United States House of Representatives are best preserved by maintaining the current system of televised proceedings. Under the current practice, every word spoken in an exchange between Members or between the Chair and a Member is broadcast live. This programming informs the American people and ensures an accurate historical record. It has served the American people and the House and Senate well since the advent of televised proceedings nearly 30 years ago.

C-SPAN provides a valuable service in our democracy. I applaud you and the entire C-SPAN cable network for your efforts to inform the American people on the critical issues and challenges that face our great country.

Best regards,

Nancy Pelosi

NANCY PELOSI
Speaker-elect

cc: Honorable Steny Hoyer
      Honorable John Boehner
      Honorable Karen Haas

NEW ROUTES: OR TEARING DOWN THE BRIDGE

With the changing media landscape, Brian understands the challenges C-SPAN faces in the future. At the Cable Association Annual Washington Summit in 2007, Brian said he "wouldn't be surprised" if C-SPAN went away within ten years since "none of us is here forever, and, as this whole technology things changes, people's habits change."[13]

When pressed, Brian retreated a bit, indicating that C-SPAN's demise was "possible, but highly unlikely." His greatest fear comes from cable operators seeking more revenue by dropping nonrevenue-producing C-SPAN.

Not surprisingly, Brian's comment that there might not be a C-SPAN ten years from now caused a tidal wave of concern and an avalanche of discussion in the halls of C-SPAN. It was less a prediction or a policy statement than an instinctive observation that media formats that don't change with the times and follow the audience disappear like dinosaurs. A student of history, Brian points out that once powerful magazines like *Colliers* and the *Saturday Evening Post*, which seemed invulnerable before, ended up in the trash bin of history. As a senior staff member put it, "I think he was challenging us, that if the media landscape changes and we do not, we become irrelevant. We need to be ready to adapt."

COMING FULL CIRCLE:
THE REVENGE OF THE DISC JOCKEY

The image of a young Brian Lamb sneaking his crystal radio set into his room to surreptitiously listen to voices from afar must have wafted through Brian's mind in 1997, when the University of the District of Columbia public radio station came up for sale. Brian had always loved radio, recognizing it as his source of both income and status through high school, college, and his early media career. Still shocked at figures such as $13 million, he saw it as an opportunity to extend C-SPAN's reach. While local jazz enthusiasts, especially in the Black community, bemoaned the demise of their channel, Brian took the democratic approach that listeners had "voted" with their dials and failed to support the station. Brian not only proposed to use the channel for C-SPAN-type, gavel-to-gavel programming, but went a step further. Unlike other public radio efforts to raise funds, Brian promised, "There won't be any commercials, and there won't be any auctions, and there won't be any on-air pitches for money."[14] When satellite radio and webcasting came along, C-SPAN went international with its radio programming. As in the early years of cable, satellite radio was starved for programming. As its audience grew, more and more content providers wanted a piece of the action. In 2007, Sirius radio confronted Brian with an oddly familiar challenge; they would keep C-SPAN radio on their service, but retain the right to preempt it for sports and other popular programming. Consistent with his commitment to broadcasting entire events, Brian was unwilling to risk Sirius radio staff making programming decisions to cut away from a speech or session of Congress. Unable to reach an agreement, Brian simply took his ball and went home, leaving radio coverage to his local station, the Web, and XM radio.

A PERSONAL DETOUR

While psychologists tell us that as we age, we become caricatures of our younger selves—a frightening thought for many of us—lifelong patterns can fall like a pyramid of cards under the right conditions. A confirmed bachelor for sixty-three years, Brian shocked virtually everyone by getting married. One of the stimuli to putting the rest of his life in order and getting married shows how great things can emerge from crises. Diagnosed with prostate cancer, Brian found a wonderful doctor; Jim Regan, who would walk him through the treatment process and buoy his spirits. While some people face cancer as a self-consuming challenge and others as a pity-party of "why me," Brian fell back on his consummate desire to learn. Experiencing his first time as a patient in a hospital and his first surgery, he spent his time asking questions. One can see him wandering the halls asking, "Who are you?" "Where are you from?" "When did you begin working here?" All that would have been missing are the microphone and camera. Proud of his work ethic, he prerecorded programming and never missed a scheduled appearance. Brian admits that confronting cancer and his mortality probably "changed me more than I know. There was a reward. After the fact, I got married." The link between the cancer and marriage seems solidified by the fact that the only two guests at the wedding were his doctor and his wife.

The process leading up his marriage had begun years before. Securing a young "trophy wife" would be out of character. Sharing a townhouse with a lobbyist for Hershey Foods had not blossomed into marriage.[15] Brian returned to his roots, reigniting a friendship with an old flame from Lafayette, Vicki Martin, whom he had known since grade school and dated first in the 1970s. It was almost like first generation immigrants going back to the old country for a bride to ensure they were getting what they hoped for. While Brian had courted a number of women over the years, no relationships developed into marriage. Perhaps, like the old song, he was "looking for love in all the wrong places." It was not until he followed his bridge back to Lafayette that everything clicked. Never one to rush, Brian explained, "I knew better than to let her slip through my fingers again."

While the term "smitten" sounds a little corny in an era of serial relationships, Brian is clearly smitten with both the idea of marriage and his particular marriage partner. He takes on almost a giddy glow when discussing it. Aside from the receding hairline and starched white shirt and tie, he could be a twenty year old embarking on his first marriage. It just took him a little longer to pull it all together.

Brian's marriage surprised his top staff in a number of ways. Some wondered why it took so long; others felt he was too set in his ways to get married. Despite the family atmosphere he had created among the staff, the marriage was not a family affair with none of his staff members invited. With the closeness Brian had developed with his staff, no one would have felt comfortable on the "B" or "do not invite" list. Brian himself would have felt very uncomfortable as the center of attention, albeit graciously sharing it with his bride.

All of Brian's staff were happy about his change in marital status and found having a newlywed boss a new vehicle for kidding him. Every holiday became a time to give Brian hints on what to do to make it special. One staff member wondered "how Brian felt in his new house on Halloween handing out candy, rather than turning out the lights in his townhouse." Becoming a homeowner for the first time in his sixties created another source of wonderment with thoughts like, "I just can't imagine Brian mowing the lawn," or "I have never seen anyone pulling crab grass in a white shirt and blue suit. I wonder what kind of tie goes with lawn work?"

Key decision makers at C-SPAN found a special benefit in Brian's marriage. New demands forced more balance into his life, less time at the office, and less time monitoring C-SPAN. "Before, Brian would come into the office Monday morning with a yellow pad filled with minor errors in C-SPAN coverage he had caught over the weekend. Now he comes in on Monday in a much calmer mood, announces 'I really like being married,' and we don't see the 'dreaded' yellow sheaves of paper with suggestions for improvement."

Marriage has a way of changing even the most intransigent bachelors. Over thirty years of waking up well before sunrise in Washington, D.C. is a hard habit to break. It helped that Brian's main purpose for early rising, preparing for *Booknotes*, no longer existed. While he exuded a thrill for books and reading, careful reading of one book per week became a burden. He admits that for a year and a half after *Booknotes*, "I could not even go into a bookstore. After over 800 books, I had just overdosed on reading and felt like I hit the wall." The love for recreational reading slowly came back, but not the early morning literary exercise. He still gets up early, but now it is to get into the office by 6:30, so he can finish his workday early and be home by mid-afternoon.

THE MORE THINGS CHANGE

On the personal level, Brian remains a willing sponge, absorbing information and musical stimuli to an extraordinary degree. Continuing has pattern of six hours of sleep every night, he keeps a radio earplug in his ear to monitor a list of program hosts from both around the country and across the political spectrum. He lusts after information and cares little about the purported political biases of the sources, assured that he can sort out the good information from the bad. If not listening to public affairs, Brian plugs in his iPod and its almost 6,000 tunes, covering everything from Merle Haggard to Mozart.[16] Observing Brian's media consumption, Jon Friedman argues that if media usage "ever becomes an Olympic event, my money would be on him to bring home nothing less than a silver medal."[17]

A LESSON FROM THE BRIDGE DECK

One of Brian's favorite suggestions is "follow the money." He is appalled by the money in campaigns and used by lobbyists. He takes great pride in the fact that C-SPAN does not need to "pursue eyeballs" to ensure large advertising revenues. His aversion to pursuing money is deeply imbedded in his personal philosophy of life. As he explains, "Since I have lived in Washington for 38 years, I've never seen so much interest in money. . . . People want money and they want more of it. . . . The scramble for money in our society is both good and bad. The good side is it creates a lot of very interesting and useful products. The downside of it is if that's all we're interested in, it seems to me to be a slippery slope. . . . I think that is very dangerous."[18]

APPROACHING THE EXIT RAMP

A staple plot line of literature and entertainment has the departed lead characters looking back down at an earth without them. In the Christmas classic, *It's a Wonderful Life*, George (Jimmy Stewart) ponders the futility of his life until the rather bumbling, second-class angel, Clarence, walks him through the evidence of the impact his life has made. Other already departed souls cannot imagine a world without their presence and seek ways to intervene to "make things right." The 1941 movie *Here Comes Mr. Jordan* and its 1978 remake, *Heaven Can Wait*, allow the main character to rewrite history. Worries about his accomplishments or questions such as "How will they get along without me?" do not seem to plague Brian. There is no question that he was, and continues to be, the dominant influence in the network. While he points out that he has "a lot of energy and I'm still interested . . . this network has been set up in a way, that if I walk out tomorrow, it will continue under . . . very strong leadership."[19] He has a group of younger subordinates with over twenty years of experience each.

At times, Brian does seem to contemplate the end of his reign. Admitting, "My personal mission is over, I've done what I wanted to do . . . It is a lot more fun climbing up the mountain than getting on top. I'm enjoying being a part of it, but it's not nearly so important to me as the early years when this thing was somewhat precarious."[20] Brian explains, "I don't think I'll ever retire, but at the same time I'm not one of those people who wants to be carried out of the complex with my boots on . . . I'm not planning to go anywhere, but I feel very strongly that my responsibility as CEO is to have a succession plan and not surprise either my board of directors or the public."[21] Brian put money where his mouth is, continually promoting his two top associates.

Brian's succession plan looks little like most organizations where the race to the top leaves one victor and a handful of vanquished. While societal dictums may claim "two heads are better than one," organization theory more readily accepts the advice that "no one can serve two masters." To heck with the dictums; starting in 1995, Brian instituted co-chief operating officers. Rob Kennedy focuses on finances and technology, while Susan Swain concerns herself with programming and marketing. The two presidents have worked together for years and are comfortable with the arrangement. They are also comfortable with their relationship with Brian. Brian admits that Kennedy and Swain "have to endure my stories, and number them." As Brian tells a familiar story, "Swain and Kennedy turn to each other and blurt out a response like 'Number 14' or '57.'"[22] The moral of the story lies in the level of comfort Brian engenders among his staff. In most organizations, one is counseled to "laugh at the boss's jokes." For Brian and his top staff, the rule is "laugh *about* the boss's jokes."

Staff members, most of who are decades younger than Brian, do worry about his departure. It is not an overwhelming sense of dread, but floats in and out of their consciousness. They recognize, "Brian *is* C-SPAN." While intentionally backing away from the day-to-day operation, "He keeps us guided. We can only hope that when he leaves the heart of this vision will remain."

CONSCIENCE IN RESIDENCE

As he approached the age when many begin planning for retirement, Brian began to redirect his efforts more than to disengage, allowing the daily and hourly activities to be run by others. He takes pride in having assembled an effective staff, imbued them with the guiding principles of C-SPAN, and is now willing to sit back and watch them perform. "I don't want to sound like I'm the father figure, but they really do know what they are doing, and they don't need me to tell them what they are doing." Brian recognizes the dangers in hanging around too long. Saying, "I don't want to kill myself in the job. Some people want to be dragged out with their boots on; that's not my goal."[23]

Brian's role as founder-in-chief includes keeping C-SPAN on mission. Stepping back and looking at the big picture often allows him to see things others miss. During the 2004 election, the Education Division launched a wildly successful initiative called "campaign-cam" in which students were encouraged to produce a short video on a public policy. More than eight hundred students entered with very creative submissions. Brian loved the idea, but asked the obvious question, "Where is the C-SPAN footage?" The obvious response lay in requiring C-SPAN video to familiarize students with C-SPAN. Recast as "student-cam," the program goes on under the new rules.

Every day provides a new set of judgment calls. Brian's presence is invisible, but potent. In the back of everyone's mind is, "What would Brian think?" He does not impose his ideas, but the choice of staff and their mindsets are infused with Brian's outlook. Brian eventually approves everything. People anticipate his reaction. They do not want to make Brian unhappy. The hiring process emphasizes selecting those who fit the mold established by Brian, creating a staff predisposed toward doing things his way. Critics argue that "there is too much organizational incest." People use "Brian says" as a preselection and precensorship screening of new ideas. Others see alignment with Brian's views on how the network should be run as both building on past success and the basis for good team building. Having the founder still on the scene maintains a clear direction for the organization, but also can dampen the willingness to change. It is not so much that Brian opposes change in the abstract or that he would counter specific proposals, but rather that others harness their promotion of change assuming Brian's displeasure.

BRIAN LAMB'S CREDO—BASIC PRINCIPLES FOR ANSWERING THE QUESTION: "WHAT WOULD BRIAN THINK?"

1. Offer fairness and balance by providing a diversity of voices
2. Treat people fairly
   - Go the extra mile for staff
   - Respect on-air guests
3. Remember that the cable industry funds C-SPAN
4. Live up to your commitments
   - Follow through on promises
   - Pay bills on time
5. Be professional
   - Dress appropriately
   - Be punctual
6. Be prepared
   - Plan ahead
   - Make sure equipment works

The potential stifling impact of a founder wed to the "good old days" misses the mark when one realizes how Brian has regularly pushed the envelope of change. A radiophile, he gravitated to print. As a print reporter, he saw the potential for cable, an upstart and shaky new venue. A legal pad and pen information collector, he shepherded his new organization into the computer age. Well-established as the television network, he saw the advantage of an Internet presence, oversaw the shift to digitization and seems to eagerly await the next round of technological innovation. His refrain seems to be, "How can we best perform our function of bridging the gap between the public and government given the available technology?"

Meeting with Brian on a new idea can be intimidating. He peppers his staff with questions, plays devils advocate, and challenges their basic assumptions. While it has almost become a throw-away line for Brian to say, "I was a 'C' student," his staff sees someone who is a quick study and a masterful synthesizer. "In a mass of information, Brian is the first to realize the A + B = C. He is a hard one to pull a fast one on."

Brian is a realist. He understands that with the proper care, C-SPAN will outlive him. Unlike many innovators, he is trying to prepare the organization for his eventual departure. He would like to be remembered as someone who had a good idea, worked to accomplish it, and had the sense to leave the project in good hands. He has clearly attempted to "wean" the organization from dependence on him, while at the same time, taking an active role in its current activities.

One longtime board member commented that he used to think of C-SPAN as "a long running play with an irreplaceable director that would some day close. On closing day, everyone would comment, 'wasn't that a great run.'" Now he believes that Brian was wise enough to "build a great theater" that has enough intrinsic value and a solid foundation that will let it exist well beyond the time when the original "director" has departed.

10

THE BRIDGE STILL STANDS

> When at some future date, the high court of history sits in
> judgment on each one of us—recording whether in our brief
> span of service we fulfilled our responsibilities to the state—
> our success or failure, in whatever office we may hold, will be
> measured by the answers to four questions—were we truly
> men of courage . . . were we truly men of judgment . . . were
> we truly men of integrity . . . were we truly men of dedica-
> tion?
>
> —John F. Kennedy

By John Kennedy's criteria, Brian Lamb should have little to fear about
the judgment of history. His "span of service" emerged literally as a
span that helped bridge the chasm between the American public and their
leaders.

THE TASK AHEAD

Brian is a frustrated idealist. It is *Mr. Smith Goes to Washington,* and finding
it wasn't what he thought it would be. His sadness focuses on the important role money plays in the process. Brian believes in the system and its
core constitutional principles. He just believes we could do better if more
people are informed and involved. He believes in the people's right to participate and the positive consequences that would have.

In terms of the media, Brian's frustration of almost a third of a century ago has barely diminished and repeats at every chance he gets that "I
was really angry about the power of the three networks. The government

was so worried that someone would fail that they established regulations to protect them. The result was a lack of diversity."

WHO WOULD USE THE BRIDGE?

Brian Lamb developed C-SPAN with a kind of *Field of Dreams* philosophy, assuming that "if we build it, they will come." The hero of the 1989 movie built a major league baseball stadium in the middle of a Dyersville, Iowa, cornfield, 260 miles from Brian's home, with the assurance built on total faith that the great stars of the game could come. Brian's faith rested more on the fans than the players. It lay in the "gut feeling that there were enough people as interested in government as I was." Although analysts might quibble about the criteria for "enough," the continued existence of C-SPAN and its evolving methods of fulfilling its mission belie any whisper of failure. The almost 30-year existence of a network, now including three television channels, a radio station, and numerous websites, serves as one measure of success. Available in over 90 million households, the term "C-SPAN" has become part of the popular vocabulary and culture. Political activists seek opportunities to acquire C-SPAN coverage. Over 50 million Americans report some viewing of C-SPAN, and even more importantly the audience reveals high levels of political participation.[1] Politicians at all levels now regularly ask, "How will it look on C-SPAN?"

REMEMBERING LIFE BEFORE THE BRIDGE

Brian's reverie of the past focuses on information and the media. "I was raised in a small town in Indiana, 4,500 people. I can remember when I was 11 years old when television came to that community, WFBM in Indianapolis. I can remember Gilbert Forbes, an anchorman on black and white television at 6 o'clock. He had a little less hair than I have. He was not a glamorous individual. He just gave the news. As a kid, I had nothing for information except for the local newspaper coverage. But you go back today, and you will see *USA Today*, *The New York Times* at the newsstand. Today you can be in a small community almost anywhere and be just as in touch as you are here in Washington." He sees C-SPAN as part of the new mix of media available to the interested citizenry.

SATISFACTION WITHOUT PRIDE

Brian is very comfortable with his accomplishments. Looking over his C-SPAN domain he exclaims, "I have lived the American dream. With no money of my own and no connections, I found others to help me turn an idea into reality." Brian is modest about his role and complimentary to his audience. He argues that "if the true history is ever written of this place, the success will be because of those people out there, the individual human beings who were involved in those early days, listening, and involved, and excited by getting information, and then doing something about it." He has a warm spot in his heart for ordinary viewers who fought with their cable companies to get and keep C-SPAN on the air.

Brian describes his role as a catalyst as "luck," helped by "being there with an idea at the time there was a need." He dismisses his critical role by saying that "if it wasn't going to be me, it would be somebody else." He sees C-SPAN as part of a much larger revolution in media options. Despite a low-key personality and an embarrassment over adulation, at times Lamb's pride in his accomplishment seeps through with words that sound like a worthy epitaph when he says, "My main motivation for being involved in C-SPAN from the beginning was to give viewers a choice in television. The medium used to be controlled by three corporations in New York. . . . Now you can get up to 200 channels. Now people are literally voting with the dial."[2] Brian makes it clear, "I am not trying to do an 'Aw shucks' routine here, but I'm a little guy from a small town in Indiana who believed all those civics teachers. When I came here, looked at it up close, saw it first-hand, I said, 'this is not what I was taught. This is just not the way they told me in civics class that it was supposed to be.'"[3]

Brian lives the dictum that "I would rather leave a legacy than an in-heritance." Many of his old friends have become very wealthy, but that never carried much appeal for him. He is financially comfortable, but his close to $200,000 annual salary is not in the stratospheric realms of other media moguls. He spent much of his time fending off salary increases prof-fered by his board of directors.

THE MORE THINGS CHANGE

Founders often come and go, having spawned an entity they would never recognize after their departure. While such a fate could befall Lamb and

C-SPAN, it is unlikely. Subtly, rather than autocratically, he has inculcated each new wave of employees into his values and assumptions. A hard-nosed cable executive talks about Lamb's "imprint" on the network.[4]

OF BRIDGES PAST AND BRIDGES FUTURE

The Shawnee Circle bicycle bridge near Brian's childhood home has passed the test of time, but the children who crossed it fifty years ago live in a different world today. The permanence of bridges is no guarantee, as the people of Minneapolis watched their modern marvel of engineering collapse into the Mississippi river in 2007. The changes in Brian's environment from those early days in Lafayette are less individually dramatic, but, in total, spell a new world. The crystal radio set has been replaced by the iPod, with various iterations in between. The three television networks now represent only the tip of the iceberg of available programming, and their share of the audience has declined dramatically. Having to cross the room to change channels seems like such a bother in the age of the remote control. The fascination with television and the utilization of newspapers have faded, as the Internet provides both enhanced formats and content. The isolation of a young boy in a small town trying to bridge time and distance seems quaint in a world of instant information where time and distance become increasingly irrelevant. Yet the bridge remains, raising the question as to what bridges the next generation of Brian Lambs will be driven to conquer.

Brian retains close ties to the bridge that helped him span the worlds of childhood. He undoubtedly will visit the bridge from time to time, but few can conceive of him living in its shadow. He has crossed over, and Washington is his home now. Just as many members of Congress don't "go back home to Pocatello" since the kids and grandkids are in Washington, Brian's love child, C-SPAN, demands his loving attention.

Bridges don't cause changes in behavior; they only facilitate changes motivated by other goals. No one forces anyone to use a bridge, but if you desire to bridge a physical or intellectual gap, a bridge makes it possible. Brian created C-SPAN with the philosophy of "if you build it, they will come." He assumed that a significant portion of the population wanted more choice and more in-depth information, and that public officials would see an advantage in making themselves more open to the public. Brian remains steadfastly reticent about speculating on C-SPAN's impact on American politics. Part of the problem arises from the fact that determining cause and effect is extremely difficult, given the large number of moving parts in

NOTES

CHAPTER 1

1. Al Gore, *Congressional Record*, March 19, 1979, p. H-411.

CHAPTER 2

1. James Lardner, "The Anti Network," *The New Yorker*, March 14, 1974.

2. Michael Leahy, "Brian Lamb and C-SPAN," unpublished manuscript used with the permission of the author, pp. 14, 16.

3. Kathleen Hillenmeyer, "C-SPAN's Brian Lamb," *St. Anthony Messenger*, 1995.

4. Hillenmeyer, "C-SPAN's Brian Lamb."

5. Leahy, "Brian Lamb and C-SPAN," p. 124.

6. Brian Lamb, *Booknotes: Stories from American History* (New York: Public Affairs, 2001).

7. See http://www.truecatholic.org/baltcont.htm.

8. See http://www.truecatholic.org/baltp2.htm#Part2.

9. See http://www.steamlocomotive.com/GG1/prr4876-crash.shtml.

10. Lou Prato, "The Man Behind C-SPAN," *Washington Journalism Review*, September 1992.

11. "Brian Lamb," *Current Biography Yearbook* (1995).

12. Leahy, "Brian Lamb and C-SPAN," p. 3.

13. Prato, "The Man Behind C-SPAN."

14. Ed Henry and Alexander Bolton, "After 20 years, C-SPAN Rules," *Roll Call*, March 18, 1999.

15. Betsy Rothstein and Albert Eisele, "Capital Living," *The Hill*, March 17, 2004.

16. Leahy, "Brian Lamb and C-SPAN," p. 128.

17. Tim Russert, "American Character," CNBC News Transcripts, March 27, 2004.

18. Thomas Meyer, "No Sound Bites Here," *The New York Times Magazine*, March 15, 1992.

19. Leahy, "Brian Lamb and C-SPAN," p. 137.

20. "Brian Lamb, C-SPAN Founder," *Irish in America Magazine*, April/May, 2005, p. 95.

21. Russert, "American Character."

22. Russert, "American Character."

23. Brian Lamb, National Press Club, January 6, 1997.

24. Henry and Bolton, "After 20 years, C-SPAN Rules."

25. Quoted in Leahy, "Brian Lamb and C-SPAN," p. 139.

26. Russert, "American Character."

27. Henry and Bolton, "After 20 years, C-SPAN Rules."

28. Henry and Bolton, "After 20 years, C-SPAN Rules."

29. Henry and Bolton, "After 20 years, C-SPAN Rules."

30. "Trying to 'Stay out of the Way,'" *Naval History*, April 2002.

31. Quoted in Leahy, "Brian Lamb and C-SPAN," p. 143.

32. Russert, "American Character."

33. Russert, "American Character."

34. Bruce Cole, "Changing the Channel," *Humanities*, March/April 2003.

35. Leahy, "Brian Lamb and C-SPAN," p. 144.

36. Hillenmeyer, "C-SPAN's Brian Lamb."

37. Michael Ebner, "Bringing Democracy to Television," Organization of American Historians, 1999.

38. Russert, "American Character."

39. Russert, "American Character."

40. Hillenmeyer, "C-SPAN's Brian Lamb."

41. Leahy, "Brian Lamb and C-SPAN," p. 147.

42. "Trying to 'Stay out of the Way.'"

43. Russert, "American Character."

44. Cole, "Changing the Channel."

45. Peter Meredith, "Playing it Straight," *U.S. News and World Report*, October 31, 2005, p. 82.

46. In 2006 dollars, that would be over $35,000,000.

47. "Trying to 'Stay out of the Way.'"

48. Rita Braver, "Washington Monument," CBS Sunday Morning, October 13, 2002.

49. Lyric Wallwork Winik, "He Tells It like He Sees It," *Parade*, March 27, 2005.

CHAPTER 3

1. Quoted in Michael Leahy, "Brian Lamb and C-SPAN," unpublished manuscript used with the permission of the author, p. 158.

2. Paul Grondahl, "Political Junkies Best Friend to Speak," *The Times Union*, October 23, 2005, p. D5.

3. Leahy, "Brian Lamb and C-SPAN," p. 163.

4. Kathleen Hillenmeyer, "From Congress to Your Livingroom," *St. Anthony Messenger*, April 1995, p. 37.

5. Thomas Hazlett, "Changing Channels," *Reason Magazine*, March 1996, p. 37.

6. "Trying to 'Stay Out of the Way,'" *Naval History*, April 2002, p. 22.

7. "Trying to 'Stay out of the Way.'"

8. Bruce Cole, "Changing the Channel," *Humanities*, March/April 2003, p. 14.

9. Cole, "Changing the Channel."

10. Cole, "Changing the Channel."

11. See CNBC News Transcripts, March 27, 2004.

12. Lamb quoted in James Lardner, "The Anti-Network," *New Yorker*, March 14, 1944, p. 51.

13. Lamb quoted in Lardner, "The Anti-Network," p. 51.

14. See CNBC News Transcripts, March 27, 2004.

15. Tim Russert, "Brian Lamb of C-SPAN," CNBC News, March 27, 2004.

16. Garance Franke-Ruta, "The Crucible," *Business Forward*, December 1999.

17. Cole, "Changing the Channel."

18. Franke-Ruta, "The Crucible."

19. Franke-Ruta, "The Crucible."

20. Franke-Ruta, "The Crucible."

21. Lamb quoted in Leahy, "Brian Lamb and C-SPAN," p. 166.

22. Leahy, "Brian Lamb and C-SPAN," p. 166.

23. Franke-Ruta, "The Crucible."

24. Franke-Ruta, "The Crucible."

25. Franke-Ruta, "The Crucible."

26. See *Journal* and *Courier*, December 11, 1967.

27. Cole, "Changing the Channel."

28. "America's Town Crier," *Broadcasting and Cable*, June 21, 1997, p. 72.

29. Quoted in Lawson Bowling, *The Great Society* (Westport, CT: Greenwood Press, 2005), p. 189.

30. Thomas Meyer, "No Sound Bites Here," *The New York Times Magazine*, March 15, 1992.

31. Paul H. Weaver, "Is Television News Biased?" *Public Interest* 27, 1972, p. 69.

32. Quoted in Meyer, "No Sound Bites Here," p. 46

33. Cole, "Changing the Channel."

34. Cole, "Changing the Channel."

35. Leahy, "Brian Lamb and C-SPAN," pp. 175–76.

36. See CNBC News Transcripts, March 27, 2004.

37. See Brook Gladstone, "Cable's Own Public Television Network," *Channels of Communications*, September/October 1984.

38. Paul Weyrich, "Happy Anniversary C-SPAN," available at http://www.freecongress.org/commentaries.2004/.

39. Quoted in Valerie Haddon, "C-SPAN: The Unblinking Eye of America," *Washington Times*, p. 2b.

40. Quoted in Connaught Marshner, "Brian Lamn on the C-SPAN TV," *Conservative Digest*, January 1987, p. 82.

41. Quoted in Carey Peter, "The Cable Satellite Public Affairs Network," master's thesis, Los Angeles: University of California, 1992, p. 30.

42. Cox Wire Service, March 16, 1994.

43. Quoted in Russert, "Brian Lamb of C-SPAN."

44. Haddon, "C-SPAN: The Unblinking Eye of America."

45. Quoted in Leahy, "Brian Lamb and C-SPAN," p. 195.

46. John R. Green, *The Presidency of Gerald Ford* (Lawrence: University Press of Kansas, 1995), p. 22.

47. Jerald F. ter Horst, *Gerald Ford and the Future of the Presidency* (New York: The Third Press, 1974), p 181.

48. James Naughton, "The Changes in Presidents: Plans Began Months Ago," *The New York Times*, August, 8, 1974, p. 24.

49. Green, *The Presidency of Gerald Ford*, p. 24.

50. Bob Woodward and Carl Bernstein, *The Final Days* (New York: Simon and Schuster, 1976), p. 214.

51. ter Horst, *Gerald Ford and the Future of the Presidency*, p. 181.

52. Naughton, "The Changes in Presidents: Plans Began Months Ago," p. 24.

53. Naughton, "The Changes in Presidents: Plans Began Months Ago," p. 181.

54. Green, *The Presidency of Gerald Ford*, p. 24.

55. Green, *The Presidency of Gerald Ford*, p. 24.

56. Woodward and Bernstein, *The Final Days*, p. 214.

57. Peter Behr, "Lamb Recalls Secret Role," *Journal and Courier*, October 16, 1974.

58. Behr, "Lamb Recalls Secret Role."

59. Naughton, "The Changes in Presidents: Plans Began Months Ago," p. 24.

60. James Cannon, *Time and Chance: Gerald Ford's Appointment with History* (New York: Harper Collins, 1995), pp. 323–24.

61. Leahy, p. 201.

62. Naughton, "The Changes in Presidents: Plans Began Months Ago," p. 1.

63. See Leahy, "Brian Lamb and C-SPAN," p. 200.

64. See http://www.slate.com/id/2157732/pagenum/2.

65. See http://www.slate.com/id/2157732/pagenum/2.

66. "Cable Center Oral History," September 1998, available at http://www.cablecenter.org.

67. "Cable Center Oral History."

68. David Mayhew, *Congress the Electoral Connection* (New Haven: Yale University Press), 1974.

69. Quoted in Carey Peter, "The Cable Satellite Public Affairs Network," master's thesis, Los Angeles: University of California, 1992, p. 31.

CHAPTER 4

1. Quoted in Merrill Brown, "C-SPAN Almost Ten Years Old, Continues to Broaden Its Vision," *Channels of Communications* 8, no. 10, November 1988, p. 16.

2. Quoted in Cox Wire Service, March 16, 1994.

3. Quoted in Marilyn Duff, "C-SPAN: The Way TV News Should Be," *Human Events*, November 1994, p. 5.

4. Alesia I. Redding, "What's News," *South Bend Tribune*, September 19, 1996, p. F3.

5. "Gavel-to-Gavel with C-SPAN," *Educom Review*, May/June 1995, p. 27.

6. Carey Peter, "The Cable Satellite Public Affairs Networks," master's thesis, Los Angeles: University of California, 1992, p. 31.

7. Peter, "The Cable Satellite Public Affairs Networks," p. 31.

8. Sharon Geltner, "Brian Lamb: The Man Behind C-SPAN II," *The Saturday Evening Post*, January/February 1986, p. 46.

9. Quoted in Peter Meredith, "Playing it Straight," *U.S. News and World Report*, October 31, 2005, p. 82.

10. Redding, "What's News."

11. "Brian Lamb," *Current Biography Yearbook*, 1995, p. 334.

12. "Changing the Channel," *Humanities*, March/April 2003, p. 14.

13. "Brian Lamb," *Current Biography Yearbook*, 1995, p. 334.

14. Interview with Tim Russert, "Brian Lamb of C-SPAN," CNBC News, March 27, 2004.

15. Quoted in Betsy Rothstein and Albert Eisele, "The Distinguished Gentleman of C-SPAN," *The Hill*, March 17, 2004.

16. Mary Ann Bendel, "C-SPAN's Visionary," *Hemispheres*, January 1997, p. 17.

17. Russert, "Brian Lamb of C-SPAN."

18. "Cable Center Oral History of Bob Rosencrans," available at www.cablecenter.com.

19. Quoted in Leahy, "Brian Lamb and C-SPAN," unpublished manuscript used with permission of the author, p. 226.

20. Russert, "Brian Lamb of C-SPAN."

21. Bendel, "C-SPAN's Visionary."

22. Kathy Haley, "A Revolutionary Idea," *Multi Channel News and Cable Vision Magazine*, March 22, 1999, p. 3S.

23. Haley, "A Revolutionary Idea."

24. Haley, "A Revolutionary Idea," p. 3S.

25. Quoted in Richard Krolik, "Everything You Wanted to Know about C-SPAN," *Television Quarterly* 25, no. 4, 1992, p. 93.

26. Cable Center Oral History, September 1998, available at http://www
.cablecenter.org.

27. *Congressional Record*, October 27, 1977, p. H–35433.

28. Leahy, "Brian Lamb and C-SPAN," p. 222.

29. Tip O'Neill, with William Novak, *Man of the House* (New York: Random
House, 1987), p. 346.

30. James Lardner, "The Anti-Network," *The New Yorker*, March 14, 1994, p. 53.

31. Caroline Ely, "Timing Is Everything," *C-SPAN Update*, July 15, 1985, p. 2

32. Haley, "A Revolutionary Idea."

33. "Brian Lamb Named 2004 Free Spirit of the Year," available at http://www
.freedomforum.org/templates/document.asp?documentID=17961.

34. Quoted in Leahy, "Brian Lamb and C-SPAN," p. 242.

CHAPTER 5

1. Quoted in Michael Leahy, "Brian Lamb and C-SPAN," unpublished manuscript used with the permission of the author, p. 253.

2. Quoted in Leahy, "Brian Lamb and C-SPAN," p. 254.

3. Leahy, "Brian Lamb and C-SPAN," p. 262.

4. Betsy Rothstein and Albert Eisele, "Capital Living," *The Hill*, March 17, 2004.

5. See http://www.freecongress.org/commentaries/2004/.

6. Thomas Meyer, "No Sound Bites Here," *The New York Times Magazine*,
March 15, 1992.

7. Rose quoted in Brook Gladstone, "Cable's Own Public Television Network," *Channels of Communications*, September/October 1984, p. 35.

8. Quoted in Sharon Geltner, "Brian Lamb: The Man Behind C-SPAN II,"
The Saturday Evening Post, January/February 1986, p. 46.

9. Laurence Zuckerman, "The Raw-News Network Hits Its Stride," *Columbia
Journalism Review*, March/April 1980, p. 44.

10. Zuckerman, "The Raw-News Network Hits Its Stride."

11. Sharon Geltner, "Brian Lamb: The Man Behind C-SPAN," *Saturday Evening
Post*, December 1985, p. 112.

12. Thomas Hazlett, "Changing Channels," *Reason*, March 1996.

13. Hazlett, "Changing Channels."

14. Linda Greenhouse, "The New, Improved Filibuster in Action," *The New York
Times*, May 21, 1987, p. B10.

15. C-SPAN transcript, August 1, 1988, reported in *UPDATE*, August 22,
1988.

16. Michael H. Ebner, "Bringing Democracy to Television," *Organization of
American Historians Newsletter*, August 1999.

CHAPTER 6

1. Peter Meredith, "Special Report, Brian Lamb," *U.S. News and World Report*, October 31, 2005, p. 82.

2. Dan Fesperman, "A C-SPAN Kind of Man," *Baltimore Sun*, March 5, 2001, available at www.Sunspot.net (archive).

3. Betsy Rothstein and Albert Eisele, "Capital Living," *The Hill*, March 17, 2004.

4. Howard Kurtz, "The Public Eye," *Washington Post*, December 20, 1994, p. B4.

5. Meredith, "Special Report, Brian Lamb."

6. David Hatch, "Two Heads Are Better than One," *Broadcasting and Cable*, June 3, 2004.

7. James Warren, "Taking the Long View," *Chicago Tribune*, March 15, 1992, p. 1.

8. Quoted in Linda Wertheimer, *All Things Considered*, transcript, March 19, 1999.

9. Cable Center Oral History, September 1998, available at http://www.cablecenter.org.

10. Michael Leahy, "Brian Lamb and C-SPAN," unpublished manuscript used with permission of the author, p. 3.

11. Quoted in Sharon Geltner, "Matching Set: Brian Lamb and Cable's C-SPAN," *Washington Journalism Review*, September 1984, p. 30.

CHAPTER 7

1. Lamb quoted in Diane Wertz, "C-SPAN: The Comfort Zone," *Newsday*, March 20, 1992, p. 73.

2. "Person of the Week: Brian Lamb," ABC News, available at http://abcnews.co.com/WNT/PersonOfWeek/story?id301384&page=1.

3. Author interview.

4. James Lardner, "The Anti-Network," *The New Yorker*, March 4, 1944, p. 49.

5. Carol Pogash, "Government Money Forces Public Broadcasting to Kowtow to Conservative Critics," *San Francisco Examiner-Chronicle*, January 22, 1995, p. 1.

6. Lardner, "The Anti-Network," p. 50.

7. Thomas Meyer, "No Sound Bites Here," *The New York Times Magazine*, March 15, 1992, p. 56.

8. Rita Braver, "Sunday Morning," CBS, October 13, 2002.

9. Mark Leibovich, "Brian Lamb's Flock," *Washington Post*, June 4, 2002, p. C3.

10. "Brian Lamb Scores Again," *Arkansas Democrat-Gazette*, January 13, 1995.

11. See http://www.extrememortman.com.

12. Dan Fesperman, "A C-SPAN Kind of Man," available at www.Sunspot.net.

13. Ronald Elving, "C-SPAN Gets Pushy: Brian Lamb's Channel of Record Wants it All," *Columbia Journalism Review*, September/October 1995, p. 38.

14. Richard Prince, "Journal-isms," available at http://maynarddije.org/columns/dickprince/031031).

15. Frazier Moore, "Booknotes Covers Writers in the Right Way," *Washington Times*, April 10, 1994, p. D2.

16. Brian Lamb, *Booknotes: Stories from American History* (New York: Public Affairs, 2001).

17. Bruce Cole, "Changing the Channel," *Humanities*, March/April, 2003.

18. Lamb, *Booknotes: Stories from American History*.

19. Quoted in Rob Armstrong, *Covering Politics* (Ames, IA: Blackwell Publishers, 2004), p. 159.

20. Quoted in Tim Dillon, "C-SPAN's Brian Lamb Closes the 'Book,'" *USA Today*, September 8, 2004.

21. Dan Fesperman, "A C-SPAN Kind of Man," http://www.Sunspot.net, March 5, 2000.

22. Jon Friedman, "C-SPAN's Brian Lamb is not What You Think," MarketWatch, July 20, 2007, available at http://www.marketwatch.com.

23. Quoted in Paul Grondahl, "Political Junkies Best Friend to Speak," *The Times Union*, October 23, 2005, p. D5.

24. Braver, "Sunday Morning."

25. See http://www.cbsnews.com/stories/2004/09/29/politics/main646435.shtml.

26. *Newsweek*, March 2, 1987, p. 59.

27. Larry King, *Tell It to the King* (New York: G. P. Putnam, 1988).

28. See http://edition.cnn.com/services/opk/cnn25/20_years.htm.

29. Fritz Lanham, "Book Briefs for 7/13/97," *Houston Chronicle*.

30. Armstrong, *Covering Politics*, p. 158

31. Lyric Wallwork Winik, "He Tells It Like He Sees It," *Parade*, March 27, 2005.

32. Fesperman, "A C-SPAN Kind of Man."

33. Lardner, "The Anti-Network," p. 49.

34. See http://www.brainyquote.com/quotes/quotes/o/oliverwend386774.html.

35. Stephen Goode, "Talking with Brian Lamb," *Insight on the News*, September 30, 1996.

36. Timothy J. Burger, "C-SPAN's Five Interviewers: Inside TV's Most Famous Un- Personalities" *Roll Call*, April 8, 1993.

37. Silvia Smith, "C-SPAN Host Lamb's Show Not for Intellectuals," *The Journal Gazette*, February 3, 2003.

38. Margo Hammond, "Authors on the Air," *St. Petersburg Times*, May 9, 1993, p. 7D.

39. Garance Franke-Ruta, "The Crucible," *Business Forward*, December 1999.

40. Peter Meredith, "Playing it Straight," *U.S. News and World Report*, October 31, 2005, p. 82.

41. See http://www.salon.com/people/rewind/1999/07/10/chung/.

42. Don Dale, "Delicious Indulgence," *Style Weekly*, May 16, 1995, p. 1.

43. David Brooks, "Brian Lamb's America," *Weekly Standard*, November 8, 1999, p. 21.

44. Fesperman, "A C-SPAN Kind of Man."

45. Smith, "C-SPAN Host Lamb's Show Not for Intellectuals."

46. Mona Charen, "The Patriot's Channel," *Jewish World Review*, April 21, 1998, available at http://www.jewishworldreview.com/cols/charen04219.

47. R. B. Woodward, "Wonk Around the Clock," *Mirabella*, August 1994, p. 28.

48. Babak Yektafar, "Is Iran Ready for Brian Lamb?" *Washington Prism*, December 12, 2005.

40. Mark Liebovich, "Brian Lamb's Flock," *Washington Post*, June 11, 2002, p. C3.

50. Jacob Stockinger, "Lamb Biographies Come Alive," *Capital Times*, April 23, 1999.

51. See http://mediamatters.org/printable/200706140008.

52. See Howard Mortman, "C-SPAN Shares Lamb Skewers on Air," Political Life, June 21, 2007, available at www.politico.com.

53. Neal Conan, *Talk of the Nation*, transcript, March 11, 2004.

54. Lynn Neary, "Brian Lamb Discusses C-SPAN's 25th Anniversary," *NPR's Talk of the Nation*, October 6, 2005.

55. The original claim was made on February 16, 1992; C-SPAN's *Booknotes*. See also Grover Norquist, "Al Gore's War on High Tech," *American Spectator*, July 1999.

56. Quoted in Diane Duston, "TV Changes Get Mixed Review," *Courier-Gazette*, McKinney, Texas, April 24, 1994.

57. Lardner, "The Anti-Network," p. 49.

58. "C-SPAN at 20" special supplement to *Multichannel News* and *Cablevision Magazine*, March 22, 1999, p. 24.

59. Julia Keller, "Woolly Spate Shows Lamb Human," *The Columbus Dispatch*, July 8, 1996, p. 7B.

60. Quoted in Emily Heil and Anna Palmer, "Heard on the Hill," *Roll Call*, August 6, 2007.

61. Meyer, "No Sound Bites Here," p. 56.

62. Smith, "C-SPAN Host Lamb's Show Not for Intellectuals."

63. Robin Warshaw, "The Real Drama of All-Natural TV," *The Philadelphia Inquirer Magazine*, August 14, 1988.

CHAPTER 8

1. 'Trying to Stay out of the Way,'" *Naval History*, April 2002, p. 22.

2. Quoted in Sharon Geltner, "Brian Lamb: The Man Behind C-SPAN," *Saturday Evening Post*, December 1985, p. 70.

3. Betsy Rothstein and Albert Eisele, "The Distinguished Gentleman of C-SPAN," *The Hill*, March 17, 2004.

4. Howard Kurtz, "The Public Eye," *Washington Post*, December 20, 1994, p. b1.

5. Kurtz, "The Public Eye," p. b4.

6. Author interview.

7. See http://www.c-span.org/about/company/debunk.asp?code=DEBUNK2.

8. See http://www.presidency.ucsb.edu/ws/?pid=64391.

9. See http://www.presidency.ucsb.edu/ws/?pid=64734.

10. John McCaslin, Inside the Beltway, *Washington Times*, December 31, 2007, http://washingtontimes.com.

11. See Kathleen Hillenmeyer, "From Congress to Your Living Room," *St. Anthony Messenger*, April 1995.

12. Hillenmeyer, "From Congress to Your Living Room."

13. Hillenmeyer, "From Congress to Your Living Room."

14. Rothstein and Eisele, "The Distinguished Gentleman of C-SPAN."

15. Thomas Meyer, "No Sound Bites Here," *The New York Times Magazine*, March 15, 1992, p. 56.

16. Howard Kurtz, "The Public Eye," *Washington Post*, December 20, 1994, p. B1.

17. Titsch quoted in Leahy, "Brian Lamb and C-SPAN," unpublished manuscript used with permission of the author, p. 296.

18. Titsch quoted in Leahy, "Brian Lamb and C-SPAN," p. 296.

19. Rita Braver, "Washington Monument: Brian Lamb, Founder of C-SPAN," CBS News Transcripts, October 13, 2002, and Ronald Elving, "C-SPAN Gets Pushy," *Columbia Journalism Review*, September/October 1995.

20. Mark Liebovich, "Brian Lamb's Flock," *Washington Post*, June 11, 2002, p. C3.

21. Braver, "Washington Monument."

22. Elving, "C-SPAN Gets Pushy."

23. Dan Fesperman, "A C-SPAN Kind of Man," *Sunspot*, March 5, 2001.

24. Fesperman, "A C-SPAN Kind of Man."

25. Lou Prato, "The Man Behind C-SPAN," *Washington Journalism Review*, September 1992, p. 37.

26. Quoted in James Ledbetter, *Made Possible By: On the Death of Public Broadcasting in the United States*. London: Verson Publishers, 1997, p. 205.

27. Ledbetter, *Made Possible By: On the Death of Public Broadcasting in the United States*, p. 205.

28. Mary-Ann Bendel, "C-SPAN's VISIONARY," *Hemispheres*, January 1997, p. 18.

29. Peter Meredith, "America's Best Leaders," October 31, 2005, available at http://www.usnews.com/usnews/articles/051031/31lamb.htm.

30. Rothstein and Eisele, "The Distinguished Gentleman of C-SPAN."

31. Fesperman, "A C-SPAN Kind of Man."

32. Quoted in Jenna Cederberg and Andrea Miller, available at http://matr .net/print-8520.html.

33. Tim Russert, "Brian Lamb of C-SPAN," CNBC transcript, March 27, 2004.

34. Russert, "Brian Lamb of C-SPAN."

35. Brian Lamb, *Who's Buried in Grant's Tomb* (New York: Public Affairs, 2000), p. xxii.

36. Brian Lamb, *Booknotes: Stories from American History* (New York: Public Affairs, 2001).

37. Gene Sloan, "Presidential Gravesites are Rarely Elaborate Tombs," *USA Today*, June 10, 2004.

38. Sloan, "Presidential Gravesites are Rarely Elaborate Tombs."

39. Lamb, *Booknotes: Stories from American History*, p. xix.

40. See http://www.prnewswire.com.

41. "Conversations with Publicists" memorandum, March 24, 1993.

42. "Conversations with Publicists" memorandum, March 24, 1993.

43. Quoted in Rob Armstrong, *Covering Politics* (Ames, IA: Blackwell Publishers, 2004), p. 153.

44. Mona Charen, "Lamb, C-SPAN are National Assets," *Annapolis Capital*, April 23, 1998.

45. James Lardner, "The Anti-Network," *New Yorker*, March 14, 1999, p. 49.

46. Ed Henry and Alexander Bolton, "After 20 Years, C-SPAN Rules," *Roll Call*, March 18, 2000, p. 24.

47. Mark Jurkowotz, "Politics as Visual," *Boston Globe*, March 15, 2004.

48. Peter Meredith, "Playing it Straight," *U.S. News and World Report*, October 31, 2005, p. 82.

49. See http://www.knox.edu/x12337.xml.

50. Quoted in Jenna Cederberg and Andrea Miller, available at http://matr .net/print-8520.html.

51. Mark Jurkowitz, "Politics as Visual," *The Boston Globe*, March 15, 2004.

52. Quoted in Kenneth Walsh, *Feeding the Beast* (New York, Random House, 1996), p. 205.

53. "Brian Lamb, Cool Enigma," *Entertainment Weekly*, June 30, 1995.

CHAPTER 9

1. Ed Henry, "After 20 years, C-SPAN Rules," *Roll Call*, March 18, 1999, p. 1.

2. Lynn Neary, "Brian Lamb Discusses C-SPAN's 25th Anniversary," *NPR's Talk of the Nation*, October 6, 2005.

3. See Irving Janis, *Victims of Groupthink* (Boston: Houghton Mifflin, 1972).

4. Emily Heil and Anna Palmer, "Heard on the Hill," *Roll Call*, August 6, 2007.

5. "America's Town Crier," *Broadcasting and Cable*, July 21, 1997, p. 74.

6. Quoted in Cragg Hines, "Oyez, Oyez! The Supreme Court Should Join the 21st Century," *Houston Chronicle*, November 30, 2005, p. B9

7. Suzy Platt, *Respectfully Quoted* (Washington, DC: U.S. Government Printing Office, 1989), p. 314.

8. Ted Hearn, "Brian's Persistent Plea to the Court," *Multichannel News*, January 9, 2006, p. 30.

9. "America's Town Crier," *Broadcasting and Cable*, July 21, 1997, p. 74.

10. Deborah Dietsch, "Historic Event for C-SPAN," *Washington Times*, September 22, 2006, p. B6.

11. See http://www.telegraph.co.uk/news/main.jhtml?xml=/news/2007/01/05/wus05.xml.

12. Al Kamen, "An 'Honest,' 'Open' House, Where Cameras Can't Zoom Out," *Washington Post*, January 3, 2007, p. A17.

13. Linda Moss, "Lamb: No C-SPAN in 10 Years?" *Multichannel News*, April 17, 2007.

14. Valeri Strauss, "C-SPAN Buys Radio Station of UDC," *Washington Post*, August 14, 1997, p. D1.

15. Nancy Traver, "No Glitz, no Glamour," *Time*, August 24, 1992, p. 29.

16. Jon Friedman, "C-SPAN's Brian Lamb is Not What You Think," *Market Watch*, July 20, 2007. Available at http://www.marketwatch.com.

17. Friedman, "C-SPAN's Brian Lamb is Not What You Think."

18. Neal Conan, "Talk of the Nation," transcript, March 11, 2004.

19. "A Quarter-Century of Lamb and C-SPAN," *Multichannel News*, March 15, 2004, p. 10.

20. Mary-Ann Bendel, "C-SPAN's Visionary," *Hemispheres*, January 1997, p. 20.

21. "Brian Still Aboard After Changes," Associated Press Online, December 5, 2006.

22. David Hatch, "Two Heads Are Better Than One," *Broadcasting and Cable*, May 3, 2004, available at http://www.broadcastingcable.com.

23. Peter Meredith, "America's Best Leaders," October 31, 2005, available at http://www.usnews.com/usnews/articles/051031/31lamb.htm.

CHAPTER 10

1. See http://www.c-span.org/about/pewfindings.asp.

2. *Washington Post* online, April 20, 2000, available at http://wwwwashingtonpost.com.

3. Thomas Hazlett, "Changing Channels," *Reason Magazine*, March 1996, p. 37.

4. "Oral History of Robert Rosencrans," available at www.cablecenter.com.

5. For a more detailed analysis, see Stephen Frantzich and John Sullivan, *The C-SPAN Revolution*. Norman: The University of Oklahoma Press, 1996.

6. Among those inspired to run for office by watching C-SPAN were Representative Dick Armey (formerly R-TX). Bill Clinton and Newt Gringrich (formerly R-GA) both received career boosts from using C-SPAN. On the other hand, Senator Joe Biden (D-DE), Representative Jim Wright (formerly R-TX) received career setbacks partially based on C-SPAN coverage. See Stephen Frantzich and John Sullivan, *The C-SPAN Revolution* (Norman: University of Oklahoma Press, 1996).

7. Journalist Colman McCarthy, interview with James Lardner.

INDEX

ABOUT THE AUTHOR

Stephen E. Frantzich is professor of political science at the U.S. Naval Academy. He is the author of more than one dozen books including *Citizen Democracy: Citizen Activists in a Cynical Age* and *The C-Span Revolution.* He regularly provides congressional testimony on such topics as congressional continuity and democracy and technology. He has served as a consultant to C–SPAN, the Dirksen Center, foreign parliaments, and a number of foundations.